REVISED EDITION

CULTURAL ANTHROPOLOGY

FOR BEGINNERS & NONMAJORS

THIS COURSE
IS REQUIRED

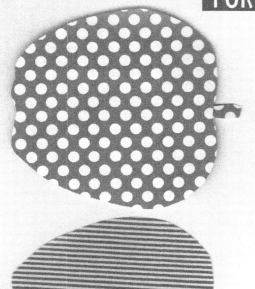

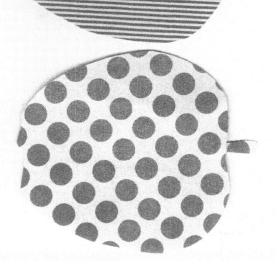

Kimberly Nguyen, PhD

Kendall Hunt
publishing company

Kendall Hunt
publishing company

www.kendallhunt.com
Send all inquiries to:
4050 *Westmark* Drive
Dubuque, IA 52004-1840

ISBN 978-1-5249-4323-3

Published in the United States of America

TABLE OF CONTENTS

LETTER TO THE READERS

One afternoon in India, a software developer noticed children playing in a slum adjacent to his office. Inspiration struck. The ambitious developer set up a working computer in the wall dividing the slum from his office and observed. Without guidance or any previous experience, the children quickly learned to use the computer. This was the first of many projects spearheaded by Dr. Sugata Mitra, now an award-winning pioneer in education. He has since stated, "If you put a computer in front of children and remove all other adult restrictions, they will self-organize around it like bees around a flower."[1] Dr. Mitra's teaching philosophy is based on allowing students' interests to guide learning and, in many ways, is the inspiration for this book.

This preliminary work is part of an ongoing project to create a student-driven textbook, largely inspired by Dr. Mitra's philosophy. Being a preliminary text, not all topics covered in the course have been included in this version. However, the chapters included are based on lectures developed in response to student feedback received while teaching cultural anthropology to nonmajors and beginners. Current and subsequent chapters will continue to be developed in response to student feedback. Teaching a course that most students are taking to fulfill a general education requirement requires presenting the material in a way that is relevant and useful for everyone. However, casting a net that is wide enough to engage a broad array of majors is also my biggest challenge. For this reason, my approach to each topic is based on cases and concepts in which students expressed the most interest. Subsequently, chapter discussions stray from or completely omit many traditional concepts (e.g. kinship diagrams). This is not to diminish the importance of these topics, but to focus on application of broader concepts. However, emphasis placed on culture's influence on daily life, legislation, and official protocols is useful for students of all backgrounds. The primary goal of my course and this text is to demonstrate the impact that culture has on our daily lives. From this vantage point, I believe that all readers can reap the benefits of applying an anthropological lens to their professional and personal lives.

As aforementioned, this text is a work in progress that will continue to be calibrated based on student responses. Please be sure to note which features you found most helpful, interesting, or intriguing. Additionally, feel free to suggest any revisions or additions that you would find helpful. Your feedback is essential for the continual optimization of this text and the unique style of this course. Thank you for participating in this unique experience.

Sincerely,

Prof. Kimberly Nguyen

---

[1] David, Joshua. How a Radical New Teaching Method Could Unleash a Generation of Geniuses." *Wired*. Conde Nast Digital. 15 Oct. 2013. Web. 29 Jul. 2015.

CHAPTER I

YOUR PANTS ARE ILLEGAL

Why Culture Matters (Even for Non-majors)

It is the year 2099. Irrefutable, scientific evidence has emerged stating that wearing anything below the waistline is damaging to your health. The Intergalactic Council, a committee comprised of planetary leaders, has convened and passed a law banning any clothing below the waistline. This includes, but is not limited to dresses, long shirts, and shaving cream. The only item approved for use is a clear spray that protects your skin from the elements, such as cold weather and rough terrain. In other words, the functionality of clothing is no longer a factor.

Earth is the only planet on which this practice occurs. Despite protests from Earth's leaders, the law passes by a majority vote. The law is going into effect tomorrow and the Council is sending troops to oversee its enforcement. Violators face a penalty of one month in prison if caught.

By sheer coincidence, tomorrow is a very important and eventful day for you. In the morning, you are scheduled to give a presentation in front of a 300-seat lecture hall. Immediately after, you have a job interview with the CEO of a corporation for which you have always dreamed of working. Later that evening, you are meeting your significant other's parents for the first time at an upscale restaurant. You are unable to cancel or reschedule these obligations.

The big day has arrived. It is also the first day that your pants are illegal. Picture your hand on the doorknob of your home as you are about to leave. Imagine how you might feel about the day ahead. What are you wearing?

I pose this hypothetical dilemma to students in my introductory courses at the beginning of each semester. I have varied the punishment from two weeks in prison up to a death sentence. Regardless of the penalty's severity, the results have been surprisingly consistent. On average, 50%–60% of students claim that they would violate the law and risk punishment. Even when the penalty was death, many students opted to "die with their pants on". When asked why they chose the risk of imprisonment or death over compliance, the most common reasons given were:

- *Don't want to be embarrassed if other people skirt the law (no pun intended)*
- *Disagree with outsiders imposing laws on people of Earth*
- *Freedom of choice must be protected, even if the choice is proven to be unhealthy*

Learning that so many people who rather face imprisonment or death over mandatory "Porky Pigging" (i.e. being nude from the waist down) may have surprised you. But cultural pressures guide behavior more than written law and can even override biology. This is not to say that biology is without influence, but that its role in our behavior is often misunderstood. Biology shapes our needs, but culture shapes and perpetuates how we meet these needs. For example, you have a biological need for food. If you live in frozen tundra, the most effective way to get food is hunting, since farming is not a viable option. Imagine that the most abundant and efficient food source is elk. Your group will develop elk hunting methods that are passed down and modified by each generation. Strong elk hunting skills are important for survival, which has two effects.

First, those with strong abilities gain prestige and influence within the community. Perhaps strong hunters are given the largest, most ornate bows. In turn, large, ornate bows are an indicator of being a strong hunter and prestige. We naturally associate power with attractiveness, so any indications of this ability are viewed as sexy. Second, the importance of hunting may also result in the development of festivals around times when elk are in abundance. Traditions, like elk-based foods and games, become a regular part of these celebrations. Now these celebrations gain new significance within your culture, perhaps as times for the community to celebrate unity. Over time, the landscape may change or new means of obtaining food may replace hunting. However, the festivals may remain even long after many don't realize that the original function was to signal elk hunting season. This simplified version of cultural development demonstrates underlying principles that will be demonstrated in more complex versions throughout the text.

Cultural Traditions:

1. **Signal insider status**, such as familiarity with elk hunting traditions or festivals;

2. **Indicate status within the group**, such as large, ornate bows as a sign of high status; and

3. **Remain long after the original function is no longer known**, such as the continuation of elk festivals when hunting is no longer relevant or even known.

An everyday example of these principles at work is the handshake. If an alien anthropologist were to visit the US, the ritualistic practice of touching tentacles with each other may seem bizarre. In American culture, the handshake is not only viewed as a requisite for polite engagement, but an indicator of character. If you grew up in the US or any other handshaking culture, think about how you were trained to shake hands. Firm grip? Eye contact? Meeting these criteria not only marks you as an insider, but also conveys positive qualities, like confidence and friendliness. We are also taught to translate any deviations from these expectations. To insiders, this ritual is so common that it begins to feel natural. If you are not accustomed to it, this seemingly simple greeting is a social minefield! Too weak a handshake, or the "dead fish," is viewed as a sign of insecurity or timidity. Too firm, or the "power grip," and it's a sign of aggression. Not enough eye contact can be read as untrustworthiness. Too much eye contact? Creepy! The third principle, that traditions remain long after the original function is irrelevant or unknown, is demonstrated by conflicting theories of its origins. Archaeologists have discovered depictions of the handshake, in various forms, in ancient Egyptian and Roman art. Some theories state that the ancient Egyptians viewed it as a sign of transferring power from a god to an earthly ruler. Others propose that the American handshake is derived from the ancient Roman practice of gripping forearms to display lack of weapons. Despite disagreement of its origins, its ongoing importance within current culture demonstrates this third principle. The handshake is analogous to the more complex demonstrations of these principles to be explored later, such as culturally constructed views of poverty, gender, and race.

EVERYDAY ANTHROPOLOGY

The Usefulness of Anthropological Methods for Everyone

"For me, I am driven by two main philosophies: know more today about the world than I knew yesterday and lessen the suffering of others. You'd be surprised how far that gets you."

– Neil deGrasse Tyson

It's very likely that you, dear reader, have enrolled in this course to complete that pesky general education requirement. If this is the case, or you are new to the field, this text is designed specifically for you. **Anthropology**

is the all-encompassing study of humankind. The many angles from which humans are studied comprise the various subfields of Anthropology. Although the focus of this course is Cultural Anthropology, other subfields will resurface later in the text. Thus, a brief explanation of these subfields is in order:

1. **Archaeology:** The best description I've ever heard of this field came from an Archaeology professor I had, who stated simply, "Archaeologists are poorly paid garbage men." This comparison is common within this field, since archaeological research is based on what communities leave behind.

2. **Physical/Biological Anthropology**: This is the study of humans from an anatomical and behavioral standpoint. It includes, but is not limited to:

   a. *Forensic Anthropology – Identification and analysis of human remains*

   b. *Paleoanthropology – The study of early hominids, such as Neanderthals*

   c. *Primatology – Biological and behavioral study of nonhuman primates*

3. **Linguistic Anthropology:** This is the study of the relationship between language and culture. They examine how language can be used to study culture, such as through distribution and variation. For example, shared slang terms across a region may indicate patterns of migration or trade routes. They also analyze how language influences life, such as how it shapes our perceptions of the world around us. This aspect of Linguistic Anthropology will be explored in greater depth in the "Language and Culture" chapter.

4. **Applied Anthropology:** This is the practical application of Anthropological techniques and methods to real-world problems. Applied Anthropologists are commonly trained in more than one subfield. This field targets a broad range of issues, from effectively aiding developing nations to advising multinational corporations.

5. **Cultural Anthropology:** The study of thought, behavior, and lifestyles that are learned and shared among specific groups of people.

Cultural Anthropology courses are often misperceived as preaching the need to embrace any practice deemed to be "cultural tradition". Some students hesitantly enter the course expecting a "We are the World" sing-along in a drum circle, followed by group hugs—not that there is anything wrong with that. The objective of this course is to provide you with the ability to empathize, or view the world from someone else's perspective. This does not mean that you must agree with them, but gives you the ability to understand their reactions.

This course will teach you to identify and understand the effects of cultural forces on behavior, a skill that is beneficial for problem solving on the job and in everyday living. **Ethnographic research, or the systematic study of groups**, is not limited to tribes or nations. This type of data collection is compiled in an **ethnography**, a scientific account of a single group or community. This includes, but is not limited to groups based on age, socioeconomic status, and digital communities. An example of a nontraditional ethnography is Katherine Frank's book, "G-Strings and Sympathy", in which she explores the dynamic client-dancer relationship in a Midwestern strip club.[1] Please note that in this introductory text, the terms society, community, and groups will be used interchangeably. The range of communities to which anthropological techniques have been applied demonstrates the versatility and usefulness for anyone, including non-majors.

Consideration of culturally informed reactions can allow us to maximize efficiency when dealing with others. For example, Microsoft employs numerous Corporate Anthropologists to assist them in understanding the needs of clients from various cultures. Additionally, medical schools are increasingly incorporating

---

[1] Frank, Katherine. "G-strings and sympathy." *Strip club regulars and male desire* (2002).

cultural studies into training to more effectively work with patients whose views of health may differ greatly from their own. The benefits of Anthropological analysis are not limited to individual interactions with clients, patients, or even new acquaintances. It is also critical in formulation of effective legislation and protocols. As demonstrated by responses to the "pants question": **CULTURE GUIDES BEHAVIOR MORE THAN WRITTEN LAW**. This principle underscores the importance of being able to incorporate cultural factors into assessments of the world around you. Failure to account for cultural compatibility, even with the best intentions, can lead to disastrous consequences. For example, creating a law that bans wearing anything below the waist is unlikely to succeed. Every semester, at least one student proposes a plan to revolt against the Intergalactic Council in the name of freedom . . . and pants. If this law were to be implemented, it may result in violent uprisings from the pants-loving people of Earth. The Intergalactic Council's decision to impose a law banning clothing from the waist down was based solely on the objective evidence for its negative impacts on health. Recognizing the cultural pressure of this tradition may have allowed the Intergalactic Council to formulate more effective measures, such as developing colored rather than just a clear spray. The ability to factor cultural pressures into decisions paves the way for more effective resolution of issues. This is also why examining and understanding cultural impacts on our lives, as well as the lives of others, is critical to everyday life.

Legislation and other official regulations, such as medical protocols, reflect our cultural landscape. The success or failure of legislative efforts hinges on compatibility with the current culture. For example, consider the shifting cultural attitudes towards marijuana in the United States. In the 1930s, a film titled, "Reefer Madness" was released as a warning against marijuana use. In the film, young men are women are depicted engaging in dangerous behaviors while under the influence of marijuana. The film was distributed as a morality tale throughout the 1940s and 50s, when the majority of the public viewed it as a threat to the moral fabric of society. In the 1970s, marijuana use remained illegal but more culturally accepted among a growing portion of society. "Reefer Madness" gained a cult following and was re-appropriated as a means of mocking anti-marijuana movements. In 2015, larger segments of the population view marijuana as socially acceptable and there has been a rise in research of its medicinal uses. The admission of marijuana use is no longer viewed as "career suicide", as it may have been a few decades prior. Presidents Clinton, Bush, and Obama openly admitted to past use with decreasing public backlash. This shifting cultural landscape is being reflected in laws, as various forms of use are legalized across the nation. Whether you agree or disagree with these laws, impacts on the judicial system and economics affect everyone.

When laws or regulations deviate too far from cultural standards, they are met with resistance and often failure. You may recall learning about the disastrous consequences of Prohibition in your high school History class. In case you have forgotten, the US government attempted ban alcohol between 1920 and 1933. Supporters of Prohibition laws viewed this as a means to curb social and health issues attributed to alcohol. It was also proposed as a means of improving the economy, as money spent on alcohol would be used for other goods instead. Like the "pants law", in spite of evidence of its detrimental effects, Prohibition laws were met with a great deal of resistance that gave rise to new problems. Illegal alcohol production skyrocketed, while venues that formerly served legally began to fail due to loss of clientele. Organized crime syndicates thrived in the new economy, while millions of Americans were rebranded as criminals. During a visit to the US, the Mayor of Berlin asked New York City Mayor James J. Walker when Prohibition laws were going into effect. This was in 1929, nearly ten years after these laws were passed![2] The incompatibility of Prohibition with the role of alcohol consumption in American society ultimately led to its failure.

---

[2] Lerner, Michael. "Prohibition: Unintended Consequences." Pbs.org.

Each chapter examines real-life problems through an Anthropological lens, meaning to see a situation through the "insider perspective." Basic terms are introduced as needed within the context of each case but are not the focus of this textbook. The focus of this course is to provide you with the ability to use concepts from the field to improve effectiveness in your career and daily life. Consider the Anthropological lens as an additional weapon in your arsenal, arming you with additional ways to approach real-world situations and problems. This skill allows you to better identify wants and needs of those around you, which paves the way to more effective negotiations with coworkers, clients, patients, and anyone with whom you interact. The ability to navigate an increasingly globalized, multicultural landscape is key to surviving and succeeding in the modern world.

BORN THIS WAY

The Biological Roots of Culture

Humans are <u>biologically</u> hard-wired for sociality, or group living. Group formation is an evolutionary survival mechanism that has allowed us to thrive as species. Belonging to a group is essential for securing access to key resources, such as safety, food, and mates. The advantages of group living have granted humans the status of being the most successful mammal species in the world. We are "hard-wired" to rely on sociality from the time we are born. Our propensity towards group living is not a learned behavior, it is a survival instinct so deeply embedded in our biological construction that social isolation results in devastating consequences. The following case illustrates just how deeply rooted our need for social interaction truly is.

The Horrific Case of Ceausescu's Orphans

On Christmas Day in 1989, President Nicolae Ceausescu and his wife stood side-by-side in a freezing court-yard. Ceausescu bellowed "The Internationale", a popular socialist anthem. Beside him, his wife mockingly screamed, "F*ck you!" at the firing squad lined up before them. Within seconds, the Ceausescus were dead. This scene marked the climax of a dramatic trial, at which President Ceausescu was accused by a military prosecutor of "genocide" against his own people and "suppressing the soul of a nation. The unceremonious death of the Ceausescus also marked the end of the regime's rigid restrictions on media coverage. For the first, time the world got a glimpse into the nation and was horrified by what it saw. Even though Nicolae Ceausescu was dead, the tragic consequences of his regime's policies lived on.

During his reign from 1965 to 1989, President Ceausescu implemented policies intended to boost the population. Having a large family was promoted as a "patriotic duty" and law was instituted requiring each family to have at least five children. Contraception was banned and sex education materials were heavily restricted. At the same time, Romania was struggling economically and facing severe food shortages.[3][4] The combined result of these factors left parents unable to afford care for their children and placing them in the care of state-run orphanages. Overcrowding, lack of training for staff, and limited resources led to horrific conditions. Infants suffered extreme neglect, receiving an estimated five to six minutes of attention each day

---

[3] Hord, C., et al. "Reproductive Health in Romania: Reversing the Ceausescu Legacy." *Studies in Family Planning* 22.4 (Jul.–Aug 1991): 231–240.

[4] Gloviczki, Peter J. "Ceausescu's Children: The Process of Democratization and the Plight of Romania's Orphans." *Critique* 3 (2004): 116–125.

when not alone in their cribs. Images emerged of malnourished infants and children living in filth, many with severe cognitive and behavioral maladies. A journalist for the Washington Post reported:

"... dazed toddlers lie or sit in iron cribs in closed, stuffy rooms. Their foreheads are speckled with flies and with scabs and bruises that come from banging their heads and mouths on crib rails. Some cry, but most are silent and appear bewildered behind their bars, with the doomed air of laboratory animals."[5]

News coverage of the plight of Romanian orphans incited a flurry of international adoptions. Adoptive families were prepared to remedy physical maladies stemming from malnutrition and filthy orphanage conditions. However, families less equipped to cope with the psychological and cognitive deficits stemming from severe social isolation. Researchers found that the prolonged stress of early social deprivation altered structural development of the brain, resulting long-term cognitive and behavioral deficits. Although placement of orphans in healthier environments led to some recovery, behavioral disturbances caused by structural abnormalities in the brain were persistent and more difficult to resolve.[6]

The tragic case of Romania's orphans demonstrates the biological roots and importance of sociality. Social interaction is as essential to our health as food and water. It not only aids in healthy physical development of neurological structures, but also lays the groundwork for the ability to recognize the social cues and boundaries necessary for functional relationships. Cooperative relationships are the building blocks of successful group living. The ability to function within a group relies on recognizing and conforming to social standards. Failure to do so results in isolation and greatly hinders survival.

PART I: CULTURE CLUB

One of Us

"Gooble gobble! We accept her! One of us! One of us!"

– Freaks (1932)[7]

In this section, the cultural criteria used to form and identify groups are discussed. Group formation is a biologically driven means of survival, since it grants you access to the group's resources. Limiting membership to these groups is also a means of survival, as it regulates and sustains the availability of these resources. The biological underpinning of this behavior is supported by the Dunbar Number, a correlation between average group size among primates and the volume of the brain's neocortex. The neocortex is linked to functions that are necessary to manage social relationships. In other words, larger neocortex indicates larger group size. According to the Dunbar Number, the human brain is constructed to manage an average of 150 reciprocal relationships at a time.[8] "Reciprocal" means that the parties involved invest resources in order to maintain these relationships. In simpler terms, think of this as friends you would invite to a party. The existence of this correlation demonstrates that humans have naturally evolved to limit the size of our groups in order to survive.

[5] Battiata, Mary. "A Ceausescu Legacy: Warehouses for Children." The Washington Post, June 7, 1990. P. A1.

[6] Chugani, H.T., et. al. "Local Brain Functioning Activity Following Early Deprivation: A Study of Postinstitutionalized Romanian Orphans." *NeuroImage* 14 (2001): 1290–1301.

[7] *Freaks.* Dir. Tod Browning. Metro-Goldwyn-Mayer, 1932. Film.

[8] Dunbar, Robin IM. "Neocortex size as a constraint on group size in primates." *Journal of Human Evolution* 22, no. 6 (1992): 469–493.

Sociality is only advantageous if the group size is proportionate to the resources available. In order to limit group size, modes of distinguishing "us" versus "them" are needed. Human beings are hard-wired to "draw lines in the sand", or determine who is part of our group. However, where we draw those lines and the criteria we use to determine who belongs gives rise to culture. **Culture is knowledge and patterns of behavior learned and maintained within a group.**

Culture creates a system that allows us to identify who is "one of us." This is not to say that biology does not influence us, but culture plays a much larger role in dictating behavior than most people realize. In many cases, culturally driven behaviors even override biological influences. Examples of this are provided throughout the text and by the end of the course, you may be surprised at how often this occurs in daily life. Cultural knowledge shared within communities provides members with the skills necessary to physically and socially survive within our environments. Fluency identifies us as members or non-members of various groups. **Cultural knowledge is comprised of:**

➤ Norms
➤ Symbols
➤ Cultural constructions
➤ Values
➤ Worldview

The following are brief explanations of each component, along with examples. It is important that you understand the meaning of each component, as they will be referenced throughout the text.

Norms

Norms are EXPECTATIONS of behavior, as dictated by culture. These are the parameters of what is "normal" or "healthy". Cultural norms become so deeply embedded that they feel "natural" to us. They guide our immediate reactions and assessments of the world around without requiring much conscious thought.

What did you have for breakfast this morning? When I ask American students this question, the most common answers I receive are toast, eggs, cereal, and oatmeal. Other than the surprisingly healthy diets of college undergraduates, you are probably not very shocked. Your mind automatically recognizes these items as "normal" without much effort. When you stumble out of bed (whoever's it may be) to make breakfast, your selection requires a minimal degree of thought. Even if presented with a pantry full of options, your mind automatically categorizes which foods are appropriate. The obvious implication here is that cultural norms allow us to distinguish the appropriate from the inappropriate. This ability to quickly identify anything outside of the norm is rooted in our survival instinct, as it allows us to pinpoint potential dangers.

What is less obvious to most people is the potency of these cultural norms. After asking students what they had for breakfast, I then ask, "How many of you had dog for breakfast?" This is often met with audible expressions of shock and uncomfortable laughter. You, the reader, may also have experienced a twinge of discomfort at the mention of eating dog. If you grew up in the US, you may have experienced an immediate, visceral reaction to the suggestion of eating dog meat. However, if you were unwittingly fed dog meat, you might actually enjoy the taste. In 2009, I was conducting fieldwork on the Indonesian side of the island of Borneo. I noticed the tantalizing aroma of barbecue was emanating from the restaurant across the street. When I suggested going there for lunch, my friend paused for a moment before saying, "I don't think you're going to like it. They specialize in dog meat." This bit of information instantly transformed what I previously experienced as delightful into something disturbing. We don't refrain from eating dogs because the meat is distasteful, but because we find the act repulsive.

This example of how deeply embedded cultural norms become in our day-to-day interactions is may seem overly simplistic. However, this is analogous to more complicated concepts we will explore in this text. For example, consider the automatic, physical discomfort you may have felt at imagining dogs as food. Now replace the idea of eating dogs with the idea of interracial marriage. If you grow up in a culture where the idea of interracial marriage is repugnant, you might react to it as strongly as the idea of eating the family pet. These "natural" reactions shape how we understand and affect the world around us.

Symbols

Symbols are what we are culturally trained to recognize as representations of ideas. Since these are culturally learned cues, there is a great deal of variation between groups. This is an obvious, but important concept when interacting with other cultures. For example, pointing with one index finger in the US is accepted as a means of drawing attention to something. However, in China and many other nations this is viewed as a rude gesture and can negatively impact interactions. Businesses must incorporate these variations into their models when catering to international clientele. For example, in Walt Disney World, cast members are instructed not to point with the index finger in order to avoid offending anyone. Employees point using two fingers or their entire hand, as this is a more universally neutral gesture.

The cultural significance of interpreting symbols extends beyond the immediate reaction to something as polite or offensive. We are also taught to attach social status to these symbols, such as low or high class. One example of this is *conspicuous conservation*, or the display of eco-friendliness as an indicator of social status. In the US, eco-friendliness has become associated with progressive thought and higher social status. In places like Boulder, Colorado, where environmentalism is fashionable, there is increased social pressure to display signs of green living. Twin economists Steve and Allison Sexton explored this phenomenon in what they referred to as "The Prius Effect". The Toyota Prius consistently places as the top-selling hybrid vehicle in the US, despite the increasing availability of equally efficient and less expensive models. Noting the availability of other hybrid vehicles, the Sextons examined other factors contributing to the success of the Prius. While other vehicles are nearly indistinguishable from their fuel-dependent counterparts, the Prius is easily identified as hybrid. The Sextons found that even when presented with equally viable options, they were often willing to pay up to $7000 more for the distinctive looking Prius.[9] This doesn't mean that consumers lack genuine intentions, but that we are also unconsciously affected by the social status attached to "going green." This also means that when given the choice of two equally eco-friendly products, we are more likely to select the item that also signals its green-ness even if it is more expensive. The Prius effect demonstrates the cultural association of eco-friendliness with higher social status.

These understandings do not only affect our interactions with others, but also our own behavior in ways we are frequently unaware of. Understanding how others decipher symbols, especially if they differ from your own interpretations, can allow you to avoid conflict and even gain advantages in numerous settings. The ways in which cultural symbols affect us at both the conscious and unconscious levels will be explored in depth in the "Language and Culture" chapter.

---

[9] Sexton, Steven E. and Sexton, Alison L. *Conspicuous Conservation: The Prius Effect and Willingness to Pay for Environmental Bona Fides*. The Selected Works of Steve Sexton. 5 Oct., 2012.

Cultural Constructions

Cultural constructions are common aspects of life that vary between cultures and change through time. They are shaped by the learned norms and symbols we use to categorize the world. There are many culturally constructed categories that we often mistake for being biological or "natural." Each chapter of this text explores how we culturally construct the world around us.

Gender is an example of a cultural construction that is often confused with biology. It is important to note that there is a difference between sex and gender. Sex is biologically determined by genetic makeup (i.e. XX for females; XY for males) and anatomy. However, the categories and expectations based on sex are culturally constructed. For example, the concept of women in the workplace has shifted greatly within the last few decades in the US. Concurrently, ideas about what a "real woman" is has also transformed over time.

Values

Values are beliefs about what is good for the community and us. Culturally learned ideas about good versus bad; healthy versus unhealthy; and right versus wrong, shape our values. This might sound counterintuitive to some, as acts of murder, incest, and rape seem as though they should be universally abhorrent. However, how we define and justify these actions varies between cultures and through time.

For example, we broadly define murder as ending the life of another. However, there is disagreement over when life definitively begins. Anti-abortionists will often argue that life begins at conception. Others argue that life does not begin until later trimesters or after birth. Additionally, the act of ending a life is justified differently in various contexts such as capital punishment or during times of war.

Incest is generally defined as sexual relationships between related individuals. However, the classification of relatives with whom sexual activity is inappropriate varies between cultures and through time. Among the Canela tribe of the Amazon, it is believed that multiple males may contribute to the creation of a single offspring. Therefore, sexual relationships with any of these males are viewed as incestuous. In the US, relatives beyond second cousins are commonly disregarded and not viewed as socially inappropriate. Variations in definitions of incest are also reflected in legislation governing cousin marriage from state to state.

Rape, or forced copulation, is also subject to the various interpretations of time and space. As culture shifts the boundaries of what we view as "normal", it is also recalibrates our value system which is reflected in law. Prior to 2013, the FBI defined rape as: "The carnal knowledge of a female forcibly and against her will." As discussions of consent and changing understandings of victimization grew more complex, many felt that this definition was too narrow. Along with excluding acts of oral and anal penetration, this definition barred males from begin recognized as victims of rape. These exclusions limited potential legal recourse and resources available for those who felt victimized. The current definition is: "Penetration, no matter how slight, of the vagina or anus with any body part or object, or oral penetration by a sex organ of another person, without the consent of the victim." This change exemplifies the shift in cultural attitudes being reflected in law. Historically, American males have been taught that being they could not be victimized unless they were weak. This also translated into little to no support for those who may have felt as though they were victimized. As understandings of victimization gain complexity, larger segments of the population recognize and push for broader definitions. The reflection of cultural values in law directly affects resources available to victims. This link between culture and legislation further illuminates the impact that your perceptions have on others, as well as their impact on you.

Worldview

Your **worldview** is the **cultural lens** through which you interpret events and experiences. The norms, symbols, cultural constructions, and values learned from your environment shape the lens through which you view the world. These interpretations govern interactions with others and the regulations that you support, such as the laws for which you vote.

A very distinct example of a specific worldview is the Westboro Baptist Church of Topeka, Kansas. Since the second Iraq War, this group has gained considerable notoriety for picketing the funerals of US soldiers with provocatively worded signs and taunting attendees. Members feel that these pickets are justified and some have described them as "acts of kindness." While many view these pickets as cruel and heinous, they feel that the US has angered God by tolerating homosexuality. According to their worldview, these soldiers have died defending a doomed nation. Therefore, their deaths are acts of a wrathful God and should be celebrated.

The worldview of the Westboro Baptist Church is a clear example of how worldview affects interactions. What may be less clear is the significance of worldview in your everyday life. Consider how many aspects of your life are subject to laws made by those who may have completely different worldviews in comparison to yours. For example, picture the people creating laws addressing the massive debts faced by current college students. How many of them have experienced the challenges faced by college graduates within the last five years? How people have experienced the illnesses for which they are writing medical protocols? How you understand the world has an express effect on the lives of others. In turn, the beliefs of others have a direct impact on your life. It is for this reason that being able to view the world from someone else's perspective is absolutely essential. Being able to stand in someone else's shoes, or empathy, is easy to preach and difficult to practice.

PART II: CULTURE CLUB

The Dangerous "Others"

"A common danger unites even the bitterest enemies."

– Aristotle

In this section, the functions and importance of maintaining membership within a group are discussed. Whenever I pose the question about the Intergalactic Council, there is a backlash against the idea of "outsiders" (i.e. aliens) imposing laws on the good people of Earth. The view of aliens as outsiders translates into resistance to giving them access to our resources. Resources are not only limited to physical supplies, like food, but also social influence and power. An outsider attempting to gain influence over a group is commonly viewed as an enemy, as this also a threat to resources controlled by the group.

The need to maintain "insider" status is rivaled only our intense aversion to gaining "outsider" status. This is why we engage in actions, like wearing pants, even if the behavior is proven to be harmful or illegal. Those who stray too far from the bounds of acceptable behavior, such as being half-nude among fully clothed classmates, risk being identified as outsiders. If behaviors are viewed as harmless or beneficial, they may be absorbed by the culture—especially if it is more conducive to the changing physical or social landscape. Innovations in art and technology are examples of positive deviations. However, being viewed as an outsider can limit or eradicate your access to resources, such as safety and potential mates. Classification as an "outsider" does not only mean that you no longer have access to community resources, but may also be viewed as a threat to the group. If you are viewed as a threat, you face danger from the group and lose protection of being part of the community.

Examinations of ostracism among the youth are increasingly vital in the digital age, where we are connected nearly all of the time. Our natural drive to be included is also accompanied by the ugly tendency to share in the ostracism of outsiders, lest we risk also being cast out of the group. The potency of social exclusion on a psychological level has also been documented in numerous studies of children linking suicide-related behaviors (i.e. thoughts, attempts) to being bullied by peers. A study of 661 students between the ages of 10 and 13 found that striking contrasts between youths who felt victimized by peers and non-victims. Those who felt victimized were 2.4 times more likely to report suicidal ideation and 3.3 times more likely to report suicide attempts than non-victims.[10] The ubiquity of social media and instant communication provides countless new platforms for social blunders, as well as avenues for public shaming. The safety of inclusion is sometimes bolstered by participation in exclusion, a tendency that can drive large groups of people to bullying behaviors of those cast as "outsiders" or undesirables.

Numerous psychological studies, such as the famous Asch Experiments on conformity, demonstrate that group pressure can lead people to engage in seemingly irrational or illogical behavior. In one such experiment, subjects were placed in groups and presented with posters depicting a series of parallel lines of varying lengths. On each poster, one line was obviously longer than the others. Subjects were asked to identify which of the lines was longest. In each group, subjects were unaware that all of the other group members were actors hired by the experimenters. When asked to identify which line was longest, the actors intentionally chose the incorrect line. At first, subjects chose the correct line and often appeared baffled at the other group members' choices. However, most subjects eventually began expressing agreement with the other group members—even when they still seemed to disagree. In spite of what seems to be objective logic, our behavior is still driven by biological drive to avoid exclusion.

YOU ARE NOT A BEAUTIFUL AND UNIQUE SNOWFLAKE

Enculturation, Identity, and Cultural Conformity

The transmission of cultural knowledge between individuals, groups, and generations is a process referred to as enculturation. Enculturation allows you to gain knowledge needed to adapt to an environment. Since culture is always changing, we are constantly undergoing enculturation in varying degrees throughout our lifetimes. As infants, we passively learn language through immersion. In adulthood, we acquire new skills in order to adapt to new places, such as school or work. Even within the same physical space, cultural norms shift over time and require learning new rules. This may sound like a simple exercise as reflected in the old adage, "When in Rome, do as the Romans do." The impressive intelligence that allows humans to adapt to a vast array of environments also allows us to embody multiple cultural identities.

Cultural identity is comprised of two major components: self- and social identity. **Self-identity, or how you view yourself**, shifts along your surroundings. For example, I was born and raised in Buffalo, New York. While in the United States, I identify as a proud "Buffalonian" and feel a bond with others from the same

---

[10] Espelage, Dorothy L., and Melissa K. Holt. "Suicidal ideation and school bullying experiences after controlling for depression and delinquency." *Journal of Adolescent Health* 53.1 (2013): S27–S31.

snowbound city. I lovingly mock my friends from the nearby city of Rochester for their slight cultural differences with Buffalo. However, when I travel to Indonesia for fieldwork, I view myself as an American and feel an instant bond with others who are from anywhere in the US—yes, even Rochester. The other side of this coin is social identity. **Social identity is how you view others and how others view you.** This is not always congruent with self-identity. For example, my parents are Vietnamese immigrants. Even though I was born in the US and identify as American, others often identify me as "Asian" before viewing me as simply American. When I visited Vietnam for the first time, I anticipated being embraced as part of the mainstream group. However, my foreign-born status and lack of fluency marked me as an outsider. While in Vietnam, others referred to me as "overseas Vietnamese", or not "real" Vietnamese. This experience is common among people identified as bicultural, or having deep knowledge of two cultures. My self-identity and social identity are incongruous, causing me to belong everywhere and nowhere simultaneously. The conflict between self- and social identities is not limited to nationality or race. This conflict occurs whenever there is a shift from one group and another, such as between socioeconomic groups or genders. Consider the difficulties you encounter when adjusting to a new environment, such as school or work, while also attempting to maintain what your unique sense of self. The complex intelligence allowing us to shift between numerous cultural identities also results in equally complicated conflicts.

When cultural shifts occur, due to a change in location or the passage of time, reconciliation of these identities within new contexts is not always clear. One example of this is the question of assimilation, or "mainstreaming" of indigenous groups. These are ethnic communities living in an area prior to the establishment of the state, such as Native Americans in the US. The history of genocide committed by the US government against Native Americans resulted in the legislation of special protections. Some state that these laws are no longer applicable to modern Native American communities and prevent beneficial assimilation into the mainstream. Others argue that these laws are still required to right the damage inflicted to these communities in the past and prevent further detriment in the future. Native and non-Native Americans have argued both sides of this debate with little satisfactory resolution.

Cultural transmission is occurring more rapidly than ever in the digital age, where time and space are no longer barriers to interactions. On the positive side, increased flow of cultural knowledge also leads to innovation and improved technology. Peaks in progress can often be linked to high rates of multicultural interactions. For example, the constant flow of various cultures through New York City yields a high rate of innovation in the arts and technology. On the downside, cultural norms may have negative results when filtered through a new environment. One example of this is among the Kreung tribe of Northeastern Cambodia. Among the Kreung, when a female reaches her early teen years, her parents construct a hut in which she can meet and sexually engage with male visitors of her choosing. However, some feel that increased exposure to western modes of sexuality and pornography has had a negative impact on the sexual attitudes of males. "I can tell from the action of a boy if he has seen these bad pictures. He's not doing polite things and the boy changes, gets in a bad mood," lamented on young woman in an interview with National Geographic.[11] As the speed of cultural transmission continues to accelerate, it is vital to examine its impacts in order to harness positive and hinder negative effects.

At this point, you may be thinking, "I don't conform to group pressure!" Or as Cartman, from the cartoon South Park famously insisted, "Whatever! I do what I want!" The word "conformity" often has negative

---

[11] "Teen Sex: Cambodian Love Huts." *Taboo* (Se. 4, Ep. 9). National Geographic Channel. Originally aired: 8 July 2012.

connotations, as the underlying implication is that adopting group behavior erodes individuality. The power of group pressure is often dismissed or denied, especially in the United States, where individual freedom is entrenched in national identity. This is not to say that we do not celebrate individual differences, such as development and admiration of unique talents. However, the limits of <u>acceptable</u> variation are determined by culture. So yes, in a vague and undefined way, you ARE a beautiful and unique snowflake. But even the shapes of snowflakes are bound by environmental conditions, such as temperature and humidity. Like snowflakes, humans display a mind-boggling range of personalities, beliefs, and preferences. However, our physical and social environments set the parameters for these variations. As Anthropologist Margaret Mead once stated, "Always remember that you are absolutely unique. Just like everybody else."

PRACTICE EXAM QUESTIONS

CHAPTER I: YOUR PANTS ARE ILLEGAL

T F 1.   Written law guides behavior <u>more</u> than culture.

T F 2.   Cultural traditions signal group membership and status.

T F 3.   The handshake demonstrates that traditions <u>disappear</u> when their original functions are no longer relevant.

T F 4.   <u>Archaeology</u> is the study of material remains left by communities.

T F 5.   <u>Ethnography</u> ONLY refers to the study of officially recognized tribes or nations.

6. Which of the following <u>key concepts</u> does resistance to the Intergalactic Council's ban on pants reflect?
    a. Cultural traditions are dangerous
    b. Culture guides behavior more than written law
    c. Written law guides behavior more than culture

7. The hypothetical elk hunting community demonstrates several underlying principles of cultural traditions. Being impressed by an ornate hunting bow demonstrates which aspect of cultural tradition?
    a. Signals insider status
    b. Signals status within the group
    c. Cultural traditions guide protocols and legislation

8. In 1985, Dr. Clyde Snow, an expert in analyzing human remains, concluded that a body exhumed in Brazil most likely belonged to the infamous Nazi physician, Dr. Josef Mengele. Dr. Clyde Snow was a:
    a. Linguistic Anthropologist
    b. Cultural Anthropologist
    c. Forensic Anthropologist

9. Katherine Frank's book, "G-Strings and Sympathy", was provided as an example of an unconventional ethnography. What community did Frank's book examine?
    a. Dancers and clients in a Midwestern strip club
    b. Managers and exotic dancers in Miami, Florida
    c. Sex therapists and clients in retirement communities

10. The primary goal of this course is to demonstrate how your cultural beliefs affect others and vice versa. How do the failure of Prohibition and changing marijuana laws demonstrate this?
    a. Cultural beliefs can increase the rate of substance abuse problems.
    b. Cultural beliefs influence the passage and success of legislation.
    c. Legislation can create major changes in the cultural landscape.

11. Under the Ceausescu regime, Romanian orphans were subjected to severe social deprivation and isolation. This disrupted brain development, resulting in cognitive and behavioral abnormalities later in life. How does this case demonstrate humans' biological need for social interaction?
    a. Social interaction in adoptive homes led to the disappearance of all psychological abnormalities.
    b. Cognitive and behavioral disturbances linked to these abnormalities were difficult to resolve or irreparable.
    c. Their health deteriorated in adoptive homes, where they were unable to adjust to increased social interaction.

12. According to the Dunbar Number, human brains can only effectively manage 100 – 200 stable relationships. What does this indicate was essential to our ancestors' survival?
    a. Limiting the number of group members.
    b. Forming alliances with other groups.
    c. Developing online social networking sites.

13. Cultural traditions became a way for humans to limit group sizes by identifying insiders and outsiders. How did this lead to humans being "wired" for culture?
    a. Insider status provided access to group resources, so cultural conformity became a survival instinct.
    b. Limiting group sizes allowed people to eat larger portions, resulting in larger brains and complex cultures.
    c. Smaller groups had to travel further to find food, leading to increased contact with other cultures.

14. Why is limiting group size important to survival?
    a. Smaller group size makes it easier to remember other group members' names.
    b. Infidelity is more likely to occur in larger groups.
    c. Group size must be proportionate to the amount of resources available.

15. While on a dinner date, your <u>expectations</u> of how the other person should behave reflect this component of learned cultural knowledge:
    a. Norms
    b. Symbols
    c. Cultural Constructions

16. In the US, symbols defined as eco-friendly have become indicative of social status. This contributes to the economic success of products such as the Prius, which are easily identifiable as eco-friendly. The association of eco-friendly products or labels with positive social status is referred to as:
    a. Conspicuous consumption
    b. Cantankerous condemnation
    c. Conspicuous conservation

17. Understandings of gender vary between cultures and change through time. Based on this, gender is an example of this component of cultural knowledge:
    a. Norms
    b. Symbols
    c. Cultural Constructions

18. Members of the Westboro Baptist Church believe that God is punishing the US for what they view as tolerating homosexuality. They interpret any event that leads to the death of American citizens as an act of a wrathful God. Their interpretations of events and experiences represent this component of cultural knowledge:
    a. World View
    b. Symbols
    c. Cultural Constructions

19. How did the Asch Experiment involving an image of parallel lines demonstrate the power of group pressure and our natural aversion to exclusion?
    a. Subjects frequently convinced their groups to select the correct answers
    b. Most subjects began agreeing with the groups' obviously incorrect answers
    c. Subjects exposed to images of parallel lines were more polite than subjects exposed to perpendicular lines.

20. If you view yourself as an American citizen, it also influences which cultural beliefs and practices that you embrace. How you see yourself is referred to as:
    a. Self-identity
    b. Social identity
    c. Mistaken identity

21. If you are viewed as an American citizen, it influences the expectations and interpretations others have of you. How others see you is a component of:
    a. Self-identity
    b. Social identity
    c. Mistaken identity

22. Cultural transmission, the transfer of ideas and knowledge between groups, can have many effects. One example has been increased exposure to western modes of sexuality and pornography among the Kreung people of Cambodia. According to some females, how has this influenced interaction with males?
    a. Some males expect more and are engaging in culturally impolite behaviors
    b. Males are focusing more on pleasing the women as portrayed in western media
    c. Males are investing less energy into sex with women

CHAPTER I: YOUR PANTS ARE ILLEGAL

1.	False	12.	A
2.	True	13.	A
3.	False	14.	C
4.	True	15.	A
5.	False	16.	C
6.	B	17.	C
7.	B	18.	A
8.	C	19.	B
9.	A	20.	A
10.	B	21.	B
11.	B	22.	A

CHAPTER II

THE CASE OF FRANKLIN'S LOST EXPEDITION

An Investigation with Anthropological Frameworks

"I hope you do not think me so weak as to labour under any presentiment of evil;

but remember this is no common voyage . . . Do not give up on us if you hear nothing."

– Lieutenant John Irving of the HMS Terror, April 1845

On September 9, 2014, Canadian Prime Minister Steven Harper announced a shocking discovery. Sonar images collected by a Canadian research vessel revealed the outline of a well-preserved ship resting upright a mere 35 feet below the surface in the Arctic waters near the Hudson Bay area.[1] Researchers were stunned to realize that the vessel was one of the two long-lost ships of Franklin's lost expedition. The grainy sonar image was the first time anyone had seen either of these ships since they vanished without a trace in 1845.

In 1845, England was at its height of technology and power. Fresh from annihilating Napoleon's forces and bolstered by the achievements of the ongoing Industrial Revolution, England was an unstoppable force. It was at this time that the nation renewed its goal of finding the Northwest Passage. During this era, a short-cut through the Arctic North between Europe and Asia was the Holy Grail for explorers. Success would give England control over this coveted trade route and firmly establish its economic dominance. For a nation at its peak, conquering the Northwest Passage was not only desirable: it was destiny. Ironically, the same steadfast confidence that fueled this ambitious undertaking would also prove to be the mission's undoing.

The Admiralty of the Royal Navy selected the HMS Terror and Erebus for the mission. Modified bomb ships measuring over 100 feet in length, they had already endured exploratory journeys to Antarctica and numerous battles. Each ship was outfitted with steam heating systems and double hatches installed to keep the crews warm, while locomotive steam engines drove retractable propellers. Quarters were relatively cramped with excess provisions: five years' worth of food for a three-year journey. Supplies included the relatively new invention of canned goods. In addition to basic necessities, each vessel boasted the vestments of high society. Both ships had libraries containing a total of nearly 3,000 volumes and hand organs for entertainment. This was also among the first expeditions supplied with a camera.[2] Embodying the achievements of 19th century England, the ships symbolized the triumph of civilized society.

The grandeur of the ships provided a stark contrast to the pudgy, awkward man appointed as the expedition's commander. Sir John Franklin, a Navy veteran with experience in Arctic exploration, interviewed for the position after another explorer declined the Admiralty's offer. The Admiralty initially rejected the 59-year-old as too old and physically unfit to endure the mission's strenuous physical requirements. Franklin was eventually hired after respected officers lobbied for his appointment. Despite acknowledgment that he would have difficulty traversing the terrain on foot, he was confident that leaving the ships would be unnecessary and

---

[1] CBC News. "Lost Franklin Expedition Found in the Arctic." *CBCnews.* CBC/Radio Canada, 9 Sep. 2014. Web. 2 Feb. 2015.

[2] Beattie, Owen and John Geiger. *Frozen in Time.* 3rd ed. Vancouver: Greystone Books, 2014. 40–44. Print.

he could direct from the comfort of the cabin. This assumption, shared by the Admiralty, was based on the belief that England's state-of-the-art vessels could dominate the frozen waters of the Arctic North.

On May 19, 1845, the HMS Terror and HMS Erebus left England with 129 men. Standing at the helm of the HMS Erebus, Franklin imagined the eternal fame that success would bring, but it was the mission's failure that would immortalize him. In late July, a whaling ship saw the ships enter Baffin Bay. This was the last official sighting of the men while they were still alive. In the years that followed, search teams compiled evidence revealing a portrait of the mission's disturbing end. Answers to question of what happened were soon overshadowed by the question of HOW this happened. Franklin, along with many others on board, had ventured into the Arctic seas before. The ships were widely regarded as the most technologically advanced in the world. At the time that the crew perished, there were Inuit tribes thriving in the same conditions. Having previously interacted with the Inuit people, they had access to local knowledge and means of survival. Was Franklin's expedition doomed from the start?

We will examine the Franklin mystery through an Anthropological lens in three parts. In Part I, "Investigative Toolkit," the lenses to be used in this examination will be presented. These lenses are the three frameworks of Anthropology, or perspectives through which we will view the world of Sir John Franklin. These frameworks form the basis of ethnographic research, but are useful for any profession. In Part II, "The World of Sir John Franklin", we will travel to the past to understand the decisions made leading to the mission's failure. Anthropological frameworks will be used to inspect the sociocultural landscape of Franklin's world and evaluate evidence recovered by early search teams. Part III, "The Last Resource", brings us back to the present time in which modern forensic analyses will be discussed. Using this anthropological assessment, we can gain insight into how England's destiny became Franklin's doom.

PART I: INVESTIGATIVE TOOLKIT

The Three Frameworks of Anthropology

"History is, strictly speaking, the study of questions.

The study of answers belongs to Anthropology and Sociology."

– W.H. Auden, "The Dyer's Hand" (1962)

Our investigation of Franklin's lost expedition will be conducted using the **three anthropological frameworks: holistic, comparative, and relativistic**. Each framework provides a different angle from which to analyze phenomena. Application of these frameworks allows you see the world through the eyes of the Other. The ability to view the world through multiple vantage points is a powerful weapon to add to your problem-solving arsenal. Using these frameworks, we will traverse the sociocultural landscape surrounding the expedition and analyze evidence of the mission's ghastly conclusion. Each framework is explained below:

1. **Holistic Framework:**

   To apply the holistic framework, phenomena must be understood within a larger cultural context. If you want to understand something, such as an event or a culture, you must examine the role it plays in the "bigger picture." This requires you to investigate as many interrelated factors as possible. For example, you want to study a dance craze referred to as "flexing" that is gaining popularity in Brooklyn, New York. To fully understand this trend, you need to understand this world as much as possible. For example:

*   *Who is flexing? (e.g. age, sex, race, socioeconomic status)*
*   *What is flexing?*
*   *Where are people flexing? (e.g. which cities?)*
*   *When and where did flexing originate?*

These questions lead to a deeper understanding of flexing in Brooklyn and what it indicates about the surrounding culture (*e.g. what it says about local and national attitudes*).

Situating an event or phenomenon within a holistic context reveals information needed to accurately assess situations and construct effective solutions. Ignoring broader social context can greatly impede resolution of conflicts and create additional obstacles. A common example of the consequences of overlooking social context occurs in legislation. When laws are passed without regard for sociocultural parameters, citizens will either ignore or rebel against them. Consider the failed Prohibition laws discussed in the first chapter. Despite evidence that alcohol consumption had some harmful effects, the ban was passed without consideration of alcohol's cultural significance to the American public. Rather than strengthening the nation, Prohibition gave rise to a black market industry, glamorized alcohol consumption, and criminalized previously law-abiding Americans.

Using the holistic approach, we will examine Franklin's expedition within the sociocultural context of 19th century England. This allows us to understand the perceptions that doomed the mission from the beginning. We will also examine evidence from early search expeditions with respect to the cultural climate of Franklin's world.

2. **Comparative Framework:**

To understand cultural phenomena, you must compare it with similar occurrences in other contexts. Comparisons reveal differences and similarities that provide a deeper understanding of the phenomenon we are studying. If you are studying "flexing" among 20-year-old African American males in Brooklyn, you might decide to compare your data set with other genders (e.g. 20-year-old African American females) or cities (e.g. Flexing in Chicago).

In this chapter, we will apply the comparative framework to two aspects of the Franklin case:

*   *Modes of adaptation: Industrial England vs. Hunter-gatherer Inuit tribes*
*   *Perceptions of cultural differences: 19th century versus today.*

These comparisons will allow us to understand the cultural differences encountered by Franklin's men, as well as how subsequent interpretations of variation resulted in the mission's failure.

3. **Culturally Relativistic Framework:**

Cultural relativity is the perspective that no culture is inherently superior or inferior to another. This concept is often misperceived as a way to justify anything deemed to be part of cultural tradition. Cultural relativity does NOT mean that you must agree with or embrace everything labeled as "cultural." It only means that you must try to understand how things are viewed from the insider perspective, rather than your own. Judging another culture as inferior or superior requires value-based judgments. As discussed in the first chapter, values are culturally shaped and represent your worldview.

The *opposite* of cultural relativity is ethnocentrism or ethnocentricity. **Ethnocentric means judging from your own cultural lens**. Everyone is ethnocentric, since our cultural lens is how we interpret and understand the world around us. However, when trying to understand another culture, it is essential to be aware of your own ethnocentric biases. Our cultural boundaries of "normal" are so deeply embedded in our daily lives that we often react to things outside of these parameters instantaneously, as if by natural instinct.

As a cultural anthropologist, I have caught myself in ethnocentric moments. To prepare for my first foray into the forests of Borneo, I purchased high-grade mosquito spray from a sporting goods store in the United States. My father, who had grown up in a similar environment in Vietnam, suggested that rubbing dryer sheets on exposed skin was more effective for repelling mosquitoes. Pointing to the ingredients beside the "Made in the USA" sticker on the canister, I announced my allegiance to high-tech solutions over the low-tech methods that he had settled for growing up on a Vietnamese farm. I had essentially stated that the only reason our relatives in Vietnam used dryer sheets to repel insects was due to the lack of "advanced" methods available in the United States. He was justifiably annoyed at my arrogance, so with a knowing smile, he wished me well on the journey. I learned quickly and for the next two weeks that the "high-tech" solution was not only ineffective as a mosquito repellent, but very successful at attracting bees. My regrettable mistake was based on the ethnocentric view of this local method being a result of "high-tech" solutions not being available or known. In reality, locals (including my father) were aware that mosquitoes were resistant to the sprays and that dryer sheets worked. Cultural relativity would have led me to seek the insider's perspective and ask why this method was used. This may have saved me a great deal of discomfort in the field and humble embarrassment upon my return home.

Cultural relativity allows us to see the world through the eyes of others. Being able to step into someone else's shoes provides a great advantage in both professional and personal realms. Consider the usefulness of understanding the perception of a patient, client, or friend. In the case of Franklin, ethnocentric views of Inuit traditions led to the mission's abysmal failure. Inuit practices, such as wearing animal skins or eating blubber, were dismissed as primitive. These perceptions were a product of the social and cultural landscape of Franklin's crew.

PART II: THE WORLD OF SIR JOHN FRANKLIN

The Makings of Disaster through an Anthropological Lens

"And now my burden it gives me pain
For my long-lost Franklin I would cross the main
Ten thousand pounds I would freely give
To know on earth, that my Franklin do live."
– Lady Franklin's Lament (ballad), author unknown

When Franklin's expedition left in 1845 in search of the Northwest Passage, the voyage was expected to take three years. When three years passed without communication, Sir John Franklin's wife pressured the Admiralty to mount a search. As years continued to pass with little to no clues, the evaporation of the expedition captured the world's imagination. As the Admiralty's searches subsided, search teams from other nations braved the merciless terrain alongside those privately funded by Franklin's wife. Persistence eventually yielded evidence of the horrifying fate of Franklin's expedition. As the picture of <u>what</u> happened began to surface, the question of <u>how</u> the mission reached such a devastating conclusion became central to the case. Our investigation traces the voyage from its launch in England to its disastrous end, in the Arctic north. With each step, we will assess the evidence to gain deeper insight into the makings of the Franklin mystery.

Anthropological frameworks will be used to view Franklin's world from two angles. Part A, "**Charting the SocioCultural Landscape**," takes a look at where the mission began: 19th century industrial England. Using the **holistic framework**, we can view this mystery through the eyes of Franklin's contemporaries. In this section, we use reactions to the first shocking reports of Franklin's whereabouts as a cultural barometer for attitudes of the time. Cultural perceptions, or attitudes, provide insight into the damning decisions that led to tragedy. "**Of Savages and Men**" brings us to Franklin's final destination in the Arctic north. Here we will use the **comparative framework** to assess the worlds of the Inuit and the English. This evaluation will be divided into two sections. In the first, adaptations and their role in human variation will be discussed. The second section briefly describes past and present theories used to interpret these differences. These comparisons illustrate the cultural landscape that shaped the Franklin case.

A. CHARTING THE SOCIOCULTURAL LANDSCAPE

Industrial England in a Holistic Framework

"It was the best of times, it was the worst of times . . ."

– Charles Dickens, "A Tale of Two Cities" (1859)

Two key, concurrent events fashioned the sociocultural landscape of Sir John Franklin's world: the Industrial Revolution and the Napoleonic Wars. These occurrences gave rise to England's revolutionary technology, allowing the tiny nation to develop into a formidable power. In this section, we will situate the expedition within the "big picture" by navigating the sociocultural events of Franklin's time.

During the late 1700s, England was the epicenter of the Industrial Revolution. The economic and political benefits of technological progress cast England as a global leader. This status caught the attention of French Emperor Napoleon Bonaparte, who was waging a military campaign in an attempt to dominate Europe. Turning his eyes toward England in 1797, Bonaparte declared, "*Let us concentrate all our efforts on the navy and annihilate England. That done, Europe is at our feet.*" With this statement, England became locked in battle to defend its borders from the French. A letter from Admiral John Jervis sent to the Board of Admiralty in 1801 captured the spirit and confidence of the British Royal Navy with the remark, "*I do not say, my Lords, that the French will not come. I say only they will not come by sea.*" While this statement may seem grandiose, Admiral Jervis' attitude was not unfounded. British and Prussian forces struck a fatal blow to Bonaparte in 1815 at Waterloo ending the decades-long French campaign. Victory over Napoleon further fueled national pride and British Royal Navy was seen as unstoppable.

The Napoleonic Wars threw the Industrial Revolution into overdrive, transforming the English landscape from farms into factories. Agricultural advancements meant that more food could be produced using less space and labor, reducing the need for farms and freeing up resources for other specialized industries. Since some goods and services were more profitable than others, wealth became highly concentrated among a smaller number of specialists. This condensation of capital raised the potential for wealth to unforeseen heights and a new upper class emerged. The new class of ultra-wealthy elites developed cultural traditions unique to their status, collectively giving rise to Victorian culture. The rigid formality of Victorian culture is captured in a manual published in the United States, where similar standards were adopted by the affluent: *"When tripping over the pavement [i.e., walking], a lady should gracefully raise her dress a little above her ankle. With the right hand, she should hold together the folds of her gown, and draw them towards the right side. To raise the dress on both sides, and with both hands, is vulgar. This ungraceful practice can only be tolerated for a moment, when the mud is very deep."* [3]

Familiarity with Victorian norms and attitudes was a marker of class, in this case the cultural elite. Membership in this class was associated with superior morality and intelligence, commonly attributed to biological factors. On the contrary, inability to enter this social class was viewed as an indicator of inferiority.

Unprecedented wealth experienced by some emphasized new depths of poverty experienced by many. England's urban areas served as a juncture between the ultra-rich and the desperately poor. As class divides ballooned, efforts were made to explain the ongoing existence of poverty in what the wealthy viewed as an era of endless opportunities. One of the more popular theories of this time was the **Biological Theory of Poverty**. This theory stated that poverty was sustained due to the inheritance of biologically inferior traits. According to this theory, social and cultural disparities were biologically predetermined. This was highly flawed in that learned behaviors or tendencies were viewed as biological. However, this belief did allow some to justify mistreatment of "inferior" groups. Attribution of differences to biological inferiority expanded beyond British borders, as explorers applied this common belief to other cultures. The unprecedented wealth and cultural sophistication of the Victorian ruling class was seen as a stark contrast to the "savage" lifestyles of preindustrial peoples, particularly the Inuit tribes of the Arctic.

At this time, the Arctic was perceived as a wild frontier in which hunter-gatherer lifestyles persisted as a result of isolation and primitiveness. It was within this context that the first reports of Franklin's fate arrived and sent shock waves throughout the industrial world. In 1854, surgeon and surveyor for the Hudson Bay Company, Dr. John Rae, encountered Inuit hunters who relayed accounts of seeing starving white men and presented artifacts belonging to crewmembers, including silver cutlery and one of Franklin's medals.[4] Rae compiled these testimonies in this grisly transmission to the Secretary of Admiralty:

"Some of the bodies had been buried, (probably those of the first victims of famine,) some were in a tent or tents, others under the boat, which had been turned over to form a shelter, and several lay scattered about in different directions. Of those found on the island one was supposed to have been an officer, as he had a telescope strapped over his shoulders, and his double-barreled gun lay underneath him.

From the mutilated state of many of the corpses and the contents of the kettles, it is evident that our wretched countrymen had been driven to the last resource – cannibalism – as a means of prolonging existence."[5]

Unbeknownst to Rae, the Admiralty released his transmission to the press. The suggestion of cannibalism shocked the public and scandalized the Victorian cultural elite. This influential, power echelon of society included Sir Jon Franklin's family and friends. Lady Jane Franklin was so incensed by what she viewed as slander that she prompted literary luminary, Charles Dickens, to publish a series of scathing refutations to discredit Rae's reports. In a series of articles, Dickens painted Rae as untrustworthy, Franklin's crew as noble

---

[3] Thornwell, Emily. *The Lady's Guide to Perfect Gentility in Manners, Dress and Conversation.* New York: Derby & Jackson, 1856. Print.

[4] van Peenen, Paul. "Review of *Fatal Passage: The Untold Story of John Rae, the Arctic Adventurer Who Discovered the Fate of Franklin.*" Rend Lake College. N.d. Web. 20 Mar. 2015.

[5] Leslie, Frank. *Frank Leslie's New York Journal.* Vol. 1, Jan. 1855: 40. Print.

heroes, and the Inuit as compulsive liars. Not only did he dismiss the credibility of Rae's informants, he also attributed evidence of cannibalism to the "savagery" of the Inuit. Considering the sociocultural landscape of Franklin's time, it is little surprise that Dickens' portrayals of the Inuit as biologically inferior primitives were readily accepted.[6] Lady Franklin and Dickens' campaign successfully discredited Rae, whose reputation and standing in English society never recovered. However, later evidence proved the truth of Rae's findings and Inuit testimonies undeniable.

B. OF SAVAGES AND MEN

Human Variation in a Comparative Framework

A common question in response to Inuit testimonies is why they did not attempt to save the starving men. To understand this, we must examine the circumstances shaping the Inuit world and interactions with Franklin's crew. In this section, we will apply the **comparative** framework to examine the gap between the worlds of the Inuit and Franklin's crew from two angles. First, we will examine the role of adaptation and how it gives rise to cultural differences. Second, a comparison will be made between past and present theories used to explain variation between groups of people. Through this comparative framework, we can begin to understand the fate of Franklin's crew.

Part I: Means and Modes of Adaptation

Adaptations are how people survive within a landscape; this includes methods of acquiring food and coping with the environment. Humans have the most expansive geographical distribution of any primate on earth. Our incredible ability to adapt gives rise to success, as well as seemingly infinite diversity. This is no small feat, as every environment presents a multitude of factors in unique permutations to which we must adapt. In general, all cultures arise from varying approaches to coping with three primary components of the landscape:

1. *Physical features (e.g. topography, climate, etc.)*
2. *Flora and fauna (i.e. plants and animals)*
3. *Other people (e.g. population density, neighboring communities, etc.).*

We have two primary **means of adaptation**: biological and cultural. The combination of these factors has allowed humans to conquer an astounding array of environments.

From a biological standpoint, human populations adjust to certain environments through natural selection. **Natural selection** is a process by which advantageous traits become common within a population. Advantageous traits, such as skin color or skeletal structure, are largely random or due to mutation. On a small scale, consider the random variations that occur between siblings, despite sharing the same parents. A greater chance of survival increases the likelihood of producing offspring, which then translates into the advantageous trait being passed along to following generations. Over many generations, this trait becomes common and serves as a biological adaptation for the living conditions. An obvious example of this is the range of skin color common to different regions of the world. Sunlight delivers essential Vitamin D as well as harmful ultraviolet (UV) rays. Populations near the equator are subject to intense sunlight providing an abundance of Vitamin D, along with UV rays. The trait for dark skin offers protection since it is not as sensitive

---

[6] Hill, Jen. *White Horizon: The Arctic in the Nineteenth-Century British Imagination*. Albany: State University of New York Press, 2008. 123–129. Print.

to UV rays as readily as lighter skin. Thus, the trait for darker skin is more common to populations living near the equator. On the contrary, populations further from the equator do not receive as much sunlight, and Vitamin D is sparse. Thus, lighter skin enables individuals to obtain as much Vitamin D as possible in spite of limited availability.

Cultural adaptations are learned behaviors and skills that allow individuals to survive within an environment. This category includes any skills or techniques that are learned, rather than innate. It also includes technology, such as clothing or weapons. One example of cultural adaptation to population density is captured in the dichotomous views of individualism in Japan and the United States. Japan's population is confined to islands composed of 144,724 square miles (374,834 km) of land. The United States covers an expansive 3,537,500 square miles (9,161,966 sq. km), an area approximately 24 times larger than that of Japan. Although population density is just one of many factors shaping cultural attitudes, available living space plays a significant role in the adaptations manifested. The Japanese mindset emphasizes the importance of community above the individual, as demonstrated in the traditional caveat: *the protruding nail gets hammered down.* This is counter to the American focus on individuality, as evidenced by the old adage: *the squeaky wheel gets the grease.* This implies that voicing individual needs or wants is not only positive, but will be rewarded. To many Americans, the Japanese attitude may seem oppressive. However, it is vital for maintaining peace in limited, often crowded conditions. This cultural norm contributed to the orderly response and near-absence of crime in communities devastated by the 2011 tsunami. This contrasted with the riots and looting that occurred hours after Hurricane Sandy ravaged New York City in 2012. American emphasis on self over group stems, in part, from the broader amount of space available to individuals. Although maladaptive in the chaos of Hurricane Sandy's wake, it also contributes to a willingness to take risks that lead to innovation. On the other side of the coin, the Japanese cultural bias against individualism may also lead suppression of new ideas. In 2012, *The New York Times* reported that Japanese entrepreneurs struggled to find investors due to risk-aversion.[7] Cultural adaptations formed in order to maximize efficiency within the environment may become maladaptive when the physical or social landscape changes. When this occurs, cultural shifts also occur to meet these needs. This adaptability is the bedrock of humankind's success. On the contrary, failure to adjust to the environment can spell disaster.

The combination of biological and cultural adaptations to varied environments creates a foundation upon which differences between groups arise. The Inuit tribes, encountered by Franklin's crew, provide an example of these adaptations that have allowed them to survive in the harshest environment. On a biological level, the Inuit people have retained the trait for darker skin. This may seem illogical, due to the region's distance from the equator and extended periods without sunlight. Nevertheless, the snowy, white terrain reflects large amounts of UV rays. Thus, darker skin serves as a natural defense from its harmful effects. However, this advantage also decreases absorption of Vitamin D. The Inuit overcame this biological limitation through a cultural adaptation: a diet high in fat, a rich source of Vitamin D. Such adaptations developed over many generations allowed the Inuit to thrive in the unforgiving tundra that eradicated Franklin's crew.

It is important to note that the bulk of differences arise from cultural adaptations, rather than biological variation. Modes of adaptation, or systems of survival, influence social structure and give rise to cultural traditions. Generally speaking, increased surplus allows for a larger population, giving rise to more specialization and more social inequality (**Fig. 1**). Cultures are further refined by adaptations to the consequences of unique historical events (**Fig. 3**). **Modes of adaptation fall into three major categories: preindustrial,**

---

[7] Tabuchi, Hiroko. "Japan's New Tech Generation." *The New York Times.* 4 Oct. 2012: B1. Print.

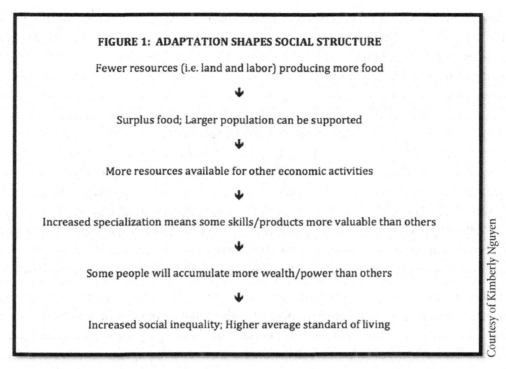

FIGURE 1: ADAPTATION SHAPES SOCIAL STRUCTURE

Fewer resources (i.e. land and labor) producing more food

⬇

Surplus food; Larger population can be supported

⬇

More resources available for other economic activities

⬇

Increased specialization means some skills/products more valuable than others

⬇

Some people will accumulate more wealth/power than others

⬇

Increased social inequality; Higher average standard of living

Courtesy of Kimberly Nguyen

Figure 1: How economics shapes social structure

industrial, and postindustrial. Many of the exotic cultures encountered by European explorers were engaging in preindustrial adaptations. Cultures deemed as undeveloped or "savage," including the Inuit, were those practicing modes of adaptation that seemed archaic to a nation in the throes of industrialization.

Preindustrial modes of adaptation include: hunting and gathering, pastoralism, and agriculture. These are adaptations in which the majority of resources, such as labor and time, are invested in food production. **Hunting and gathering** is practiced in regions where farming is not a viable option, such as in deserts or frozen tundra. Such terrains yield limited food sources and result in little to no surplus. These conditions restrict group size to what the environment can support. Small group size and lack of surplus requires that everyone in the group contribute to food acquisition in some way, resulting in a generalized labor pool with little specialization. For example, hunting caribou provides more food and is more valuable than being able to gather moss. In a small hunter-gatherer group, there needs to be more than one person (specialist) who knows how to hunt caribou. Additionally, each person must be able to contribute in numerous ways. Hence, there is little specialization, resulting in the least amount of social inequality. The Inuit tribes of the Arctic were and continue to be hunter-gatherers. This mode of adaptation affected their interactions with Franklin's crew in ways to be discussed later in the chapter.

Another preindustrial mode of adaptation is **pastoralism**, in which groups rely primarily on livestock for sustenance. In similar fashion to hunter-gatherers, group size is relatively limited based on availability of resources in the environment. However, parameters are set by food and water supply for livestock. Pastoralists display some social inequality, usually informed by who controls or owns the livestock. The Maasai people of Kenya are modern-day pastoralists. Livestock is owned by the men, so social inequality is most apparent along gender lines.

The third type of preindustrial adaptation is **agriculture**, or farming. There are two broad categories of agriculture: horticulture and intensive agriculture. For our purposes, the primary difference between these classifications is the amount of surplus produced. Horticulture relies primarily on hand tools, while intensive agriculturalists implement livestock and machinery. Horticulture provides some surplus, allowing for a moderately sized population, and giving rise to some social inequality. This mode of adaptation requires a large amount of land, whereas intensive agriculture's success hinges on reusing the same amount of land to produce more food. Both forms of agriculture produce more food than is needed by each unit (i.e. family), resulting in the accumulation of surplus. Extra food translates into larger group sizes, since the environment can now support more people. Surplus allows a variety of needs to be met without needing to produce it, so farmers can specialize by focusing on different crops. Since some crops are more valuable than others, this also gives rise to increased social inequality. Indonesian rice farmers are an example of the structural shift resulting from agriculture. The nation of Indonesia has a population of approximately 250 million people inhabiting over 6,000 islands. Rice is the nation's primary food staple, with each person estimated to consume 306 pounds (139 kg) per year. Astonishingly, nearly 60% of the nation's rice comes from the island of Java, an island only comprising about 9% of Indonesia's total landmass. Java's dominance in rice production contributes to the concentration of wealth and power on this island, which is also home to the nation's capital of Jakarta.

Industrialism is a mode of adaption defined by a shift of resources from food production to manufacturing. The ability to produce a greater amount of food with a smaller amount of resources (e.g. space, labor) results in an increased population. With a larger population, but fewer people needed for food production, individuals can focus resources on other areas of life giving rise to increased specialization. Since some industries are more profitable than others, this creates an increase in social inequality. The concurrent trend of increased specialization and social inequality was exemplified by the rise of the Victorian elite during the Industrial Revolution.

The transformation of the sociocultural landscape produced within Franklin's era was little more than a wardrobe change compared to the extreme makeover of today's **postindustrial** era. Postindustrialism marks the shift away from manufacturing, instead allocating resource toward technology involved in service and communication. This adaptation requires the least amount of resource and yields the greatest amount of food. An example of this is the modern-day United States, where less than 1% of its 313 million citizens identify as farmers.[8] However, jobs in the service industry (e.g. call centers, food service) accounted for approximately 80% of all employment in 2012.[9] Immense surplus supports unconstrained population growth. With a larger population and less need for resources (i.e. labor, land) dedicated to food production, more people are able to specialize in a wider variety of goods and services. A broader spectrum of specialization also leads to greater divides between socioeconomic groups, translating into a larger gap between the wealthiest and poorest citizens. On the positive side, the average standard of living is higher than that in preindustrial and industrial societies. Consider what it means to be poor in the United States versus in a developing nation. In the United States, access to safe drinking water is generally not a concern as it is in developing nations. This basic necessity is available to every citizen, regardless of poverty level. This is not to diminish the struggles of the poor in the United States, but to illustrate the disparity between struggles of the poor in postindustrial nations in comparison to others.

Modes of adaptation shape the social structure and cultural values, giving rise to endless variation between groups. Explorers of the 19th century interpreted the egalitarian social structure of the Inuit as the "innocence" of simple-minded people, lacking in desire or ambition. However, egalitarianism is more efficient

---

[8] "Demographics." *EPA*. Environmental Protection Agency, 14 Apr. 2013. Web. 11 Mar. 2015.

[9] "Employment by Major Industry Sector." *U.S. Bureau of Labor Statistics*. U.S. Bureau of Labor Statistics, Dec. 2013. Web. 11 Mar. 2015.

for survival among hunter-gatherers. Drive and ambition are manifested in other ways in Inuit culture, a notion that Dr. John Rae attempted to present in response to Dickens' attacks on their credibility. However, the idea of Inuits bearing moral similarities to the English was not cohesive in an era when preindustrial groups were viewed as biologically inferior. This perception does not mean that the British were malicious, but was a product of the sociocultural values shaped by industrialism. Remember that adaptations shape cultural values, which form the parameters of what we see as normal. In the setting of industrialized 19th century England, the coexistence of the ultra-wealthy Victorian elite and the impoverished working classes influenced cultural values. Mass production of goods reduced the need for interdependence, making the accumulation of wealth for one individual both possible and desirable. The wealthy were viewed as a symbol of potential and possibility. By the same token, the poor became representative of social deviance and inferiority. They were a living cautionary tale to the middle and upper classes. Cultural values stemming from different modes of adaptation led to opposite interpretations of unequal resource distribution. Hunting and gathering groups have limited surplus, which makes the accumulation of resources by a few individuals detrimental to the community. Thus, inordinate control over a large amount of resources by a small segment of the population is more likely to be viewed negatively. Industrial societies have immense surplus, which makes unequal resource distribution less hazardous and often interpreted as a positive accomplishment.

It was in this sociocultural context, that accounts of Inuit attempts to help the men were suppressed by a more culturally favorable narrative of English superiority. Although these interactions did occur, encounters between Inuit hunters and living crewmembers were rare. Being hunter-gatherers, food supply limited group size and Inuits rarely traveled with more than 50 individuals. Additionally, Inuit hunters did not commonly use the region occupied by Franklin's men. However, there is evidence that they occasionally traded with the men, providing them with meat when possible. Others reported that they attempted to help the men, but that the crew lacked even the most basic skills necessary for survival. Scurvy, a painful condition brought on by Vitamin C deficiency, was a common and fatal condition. Despite the lack of available fruit, the absence of this condition among the Inuit is owed to incorporation of animal organs into the diet. The British refused to consume these parts, leading to a high rate of scurvy and death among the crew.[10] The idea of crewmembers as less capable than local "savages" deviated from the cultural narrative of the English as the pinnacle of civilization. This informed the public's willingness to embrace the narrative of Franklin's men heroically maintaining civility in a land of the dangerous Other.

Part II: Past and Present Theories of Cultural Differences

The cultural shifts of the Industrial Revolution reframed other modes of adaptation as antiquated and inferior. Beliefs regarding the biological roots of class in 19th century England were also used to explain even more distinct variations outside of the nation. The worldview of Franklin and his contemporaries was shaped by the theory of **unilineal evolution** (Fig. 3). Discredited in the 1900s, this theory posited that preindustrial groups represented early stages of human development. Humanity was believed to be through stages of savagery, barbarism, and eventually civilization. Of course, European culture was situated as the height of civilization. Until the 1900s, this school of thought was often used to rationalize conquering groups viewed as inferior as they were bringing civilization to savages. Hunter-gatherers were seen as living windows of the past. Early ethnographies reflected this sentiment in describing preindustrial groups as "savages" or "primitives." This

---

[10] Roberts, David. "Last Words Missing—The Mystery of Sir John Franklin and Polar History's Greatest Catastrophe." *Beyond the Edge: Adventure Blog.* National Geographic. 30 Mar. 2012. Web. 14 Feb. 2015.

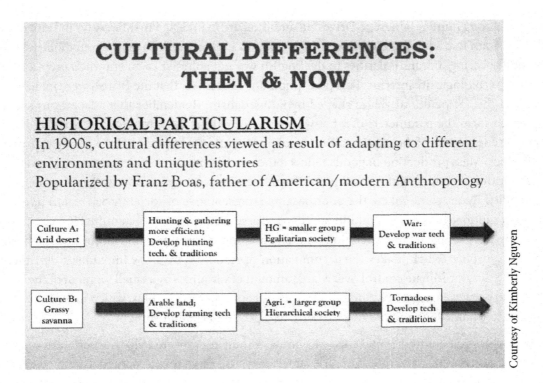

Figure 2: Historical Particularism

mode of thought continues to be echoed in modern media tropes, such as "the noble savage" in which pre-industrial people are portrayed as innocent and childlike.

In the 1900s, unilineal evolution was displaced when intellectual luminaries began promoting **historical particularism (Fig. 2)** as a means of explaining cultural differences. Leading this revolutionary school of thought was Franz Boas, the father of modern-day anthropology. Contrary to unilineal evolution, Boas stated that cultural development does not occur along one universal scale (i.e. savagery → civilization). Deviating from the belief that preindustrial people were inferior, he posited that all human beings were biologically equal and that cultural variation was the result of each group's unique history. Thus, cultural development must be assessed within the context of its own particular history, rather than measured against a nonexistent universal standard of achievement. Tenets of historical particularism, particularly the importance of historical context, became the basis for later theories of cultural variation.

Unilineal thinking inspired nationalistic faith in British superiority over the rest of the world. This belief gave Lady Franklin hope that her husband may still be alive. This idea was extinguished in 1859, based on irrefutable evidence discovered by one of her privately funded expeditions. Led by Captain Francis McClintock, search teams discovered a cairn at Victory Point on King William Island. Nestled inside the stone pile was a tin can containing what became known as the "Victory Point Letter." Two reports, also the last words of Franklin's crew, were scrawled on official paper. The first, dated May 1847, stated that the ships were icebound but all were well. In April 1848, a final report stated that the ships had been stuck in ice for 20 months and 24 men had died. It was in this report that Lady Franklin learned that her husband died suddenly aboard the HMS Erebus on June 11, 1847.[11] With Franklin dead and the ships hopelessly icebound, Captain Francis Crozier

---

[11] Rondeau, Robin M. "The wrecks of Franklin's ships Erebus and Terror; their likely location and the cause of failure of previous search expeditions." *The Journal of the Hakluyt Society* (www.hakluyt.com), Mar. 2010, 1–11. Web. 20 February 2015.

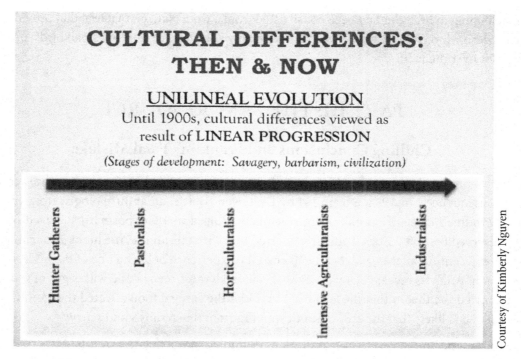

CULTURAL DIFFERENCES: THEN & NOW

UNILINEAL EVOLUTION

Until 1900s, cultural differences viewed as result of LINEAR PROGRESSION

(Stages of development: Savagery, barbarism, civilization)

Hunter Gatherers — Pastoralists — Horticulturalists — Intensive Agriculturalists — Industrialists

Courtesy of Kimberly Nguyen

Figure 3: Unilineal Evolution

took command and made the desperate decision to set off on foot with the 105 remaining crewmembers in search of help. Every man would perish on this journey, leaving a trail of artifacts and Inuit accounts as evidence of their horrific final days.

Like Dr. John Rae, the McClintock expedition also encountered Inuits from whom they were able to purchase relics of the Franklin crew. The Inuit provided accounts of white men starving to death, corroborating Rae's reports. McClintock's findings led to the puzzling conclusion that despite ample provisions, starvation had been the primary cause of the crew's death. Among artifacts recovered were unopened cans, suggesting the torturous predicament of starving while surrounded by food. The relinquishment of this high-tech food source has been a point of interest for many researchers, fueling suspicions that food contamination played a key role in the crew's demise. Canned food was a relatively new technology and lead was commonly used for soldering. Inventory missing from a wooden medical chest indicates that indigestion was the most common complaint. Coupled with the abandonment of canned goods, this suggests that the men eventually realized that the canned food was tainted. Not anticipating the loss of this major provision, they were ill prepared to cope with this problem.

One of McClintock's eerier findings was a lifeboat in which two skeletons sat awaiting rescue alongside a pile of items that were not conducive to Arctic travel, such as button polish and silverware. The peculiar assortment of items indicated that the crew's final hours were marked by chaos and confusion, likely exacerbated by the psychological strain of starvation and illness. If the strange array of artifacts revealed the crew's chaotic final days, the absence of other items points to a mission that was doomed from the start. While the men had literature, musical instruments, and fine silverware; they did not have lightweight sleds, weapons for hunting large game, or clothing to withstand the elements. When the crew abandoned ship, many attempted to construct makeshift equipment. For example, McClintock found spectacles to which someone had attempted to attach fabric. Goggles for snow blindness, a known occurrence, were available but not supplied.

A mitten belonging to Franklin had been constructed from a wool blanket, material that provides little relief from the subzero wind chill. Available weapons were only adequate for hunting small birds, providing little sustenance for over the men.

PART III: THE LAST RESOURCE

Chilling Conclusions and Franklin's Fatal Mistake

While artifacts provided a picture of ill-preparedness and maladaptation, forensic analysis confirmed its gruesome consequences. In 1984, a team led by Dr. Owen Beattie, an anthropologist from the University of Alberta, exhumed three of Franklin's crewmembers. Buried in 1846, permafrost staved off decay and perfectly preserved the soft tissues. Popularly referred to as "ice mummies," the limbs also maintained some flexibility over a century after burial. Beattie likened the experience of lifting one of the bodies to moving a sleeping person. Analysis revealed fatal dosages of lead in all three men, along with signs of starvation. This finding supported the theory that the lead used to solder the canned food affected the crew. In addition to lead poisoning, it is likely that the crew's health suffered from tuberculosis and scurvy.

Cut marks on the bones were consistent with Rae's initial reports that the crew had resorted to cannibalism in their darkest hours. One of the grislier Inuit testimonies detailed an encounter with the men in the summer of 1848. During their 932-mile (1,500 km) trek to Hudson Bay's fort, the desperate men resorted to cannibalizing a fallen shipmate. After immediately consuming the meatier portions of the torso, they continued their trek across the icy strait carrying the man's head, arms, and legs. Combined testimonies, artifacts, and forensic evidence make the possibility that Franklin's men did NOT resort to cannibalism highly unlikely.

Following announcement of the discovery on September 9, 2014, journalist Peter Mansbridge issued this statement to the Canadian Broadcasting Company:

"The beauty of where they found it is it's proof positive of Inuit oral history . . . the Inuit have said for generations that one of their hunters saw a ship in that part of the passage, abandoned and ended up wrecking . . . It's exactly where this guy said it was."[12] On September 30, 2014, researchers confirmed that the wreckage was the HMS Erebus, the vessel on which Franklin died. At the time of this writing, underwater archaeologists have been working steadily to carefully excavate the wreck.

Industrialization transformed the social structure of 19th century England. Technological advancements created an unprecedented amount of surplus. This led many to believe that the persistence of poverty was most likely a product of biological inferiority. This concept shaped interpretations of even more starkly different groups, such as Inuit tribes, as "naturally" inferior. Subsequently, this gave rise to the ethnocentric view of Inuit culture as irrelevant and primitive. This resulted in a general dismissal of local knowledge and technology. When the HMS Erebus and Terror left the harbor, they were equipped with all of the technological and cultural comforts of industrial England. However, the accoutrements of the industrialized world rendered Franklin's crew helpless beyond the comfort of their cabins. Examining Franklin's lost expedition through anthropological frameworks provides a broader view of the factors that simultaneously launched and doomed the mission.

---

[12] CBC News. "Lost Franklin Expedition Found in the Arctic." *CBCnews*. CBC/Radio Canada, 9 Sep. 2014. Web. 2 Feb. 2015.

PRACTICE EXAM QUESTIONS

CHAPTER II: THE CASE OF FRANKLIN'S LOST EXPEDITION

T F 1.   <u>The Relativistic Framework</u> implies that no culture is inherently superior or inferior to another.

T F 2.   Natural selection is an example of a <u>cultural</u> adaptation.

T F 3.   Pastoralism is a <u>postindustrial</u> mode of adaptation.

T F 4.   <u>Unilineal evolution</u> attributes cultural differences to adaptations and historical events.

T F 5.   The British view of Inuit technology as primitive was <u>ethnocentric</u>.

6.   Which Framework of anthropology is used to examine the sociocultural context (i.e. Industrial Revolution, Napoleonic Wars) of Franklin's lost expedition?
   a.   Holistic
   b.   Comparative
   c.   Relativistic

7.   The Industrial Revolution generated a new class of cultural elite. Subsequently, new cultural traditions developed as markers of high status. Which example of upper-class culture does the chapter discuss?
   a.   Children working as chimney sweeps
   b.   Victorian etiquette for women
   c.   Victorian clothing for men

8.   The Industrial Revolution widened the gap between England's socioeconomic classes. Ongoing poverty amidst the nation's growing wealth reinforced a popular belief in the Biological Theory of Poverty. What did this state?
   a.   Limited access to biological resources, such as a land and water, lead to poverty
   b.   Poverty is sustained by the biological inferiority of the poor
   c.   Poor nutrition leads to biological deficiencies

9.   The view of certain groups as biologically inferior shaped interpretations of evidence regarding Franklin's crew. <u>How did this belief influence Lady Franklin and Charles Dickens' reactions to evidence of cannibalism in Dr. Rae's initial report?</u>
   a.   It was attributed to low-ranking crewmen, since most came from poor families and would be biologically inclined to "savage" behavior
   b.   Dr. Rae's report was dismissed, based on the belief that his "inferior" Scottish heritage made him prone to believe accounts from the "savage" Inuits
   c.   Suggesting that the noble British would engage in such uncivilized behavior was viewed as slander. Evidence of cannibalism was blamed on the "savage" Inuit.

10. Japanese culture emphasizes the importance of community over the individual, which is advantageous for cooperation and order in a densely populated nation. Which <u>disadvantage</u> of this worldview does the chapter discuss?
    a. Risk-aversion: Entrepreneurs have difficulty finding investors for new ideas
    b. Protocol-reliance: Inability to adapt to chaos left by natural disasters
    c. Hyper-tolerance: To avoid standing out, many fail to report criminal activity

11. Mode of adaptation dictates the amount of surplus resources generated, which then influences culture. What is the effect of <u>increased surplus</u> on social structure?
    a. Smaller population; more specialization; more inequality
    b. Larger population; less specialization; less inequality
    c. Larger population; more specialization; more inequality

12. Inuit tribes live in a frozen tundra where farming is not an efficient mode of adaptation. What type of preindustrial adaptation is practiced by the Inuit?
    a. Hunting and gathering
    b. Pastoralism
    c. Horticulture

13. The Maasai people of Kenya rely primarily on <u>herding livestock</u> to survive. Males control all livestock, so they display some gender-based social inequality. How would anthropologists describe this mode of adaptation?
    a. Pastoralism
    b. Horticulture
    c. Intensive agriculture

14. In Indonesia, many rice farmers rely primarily on <u>machinery and livestock</u>. This allows a lot of food to be generated by a small amount of land and labor. How would anthropologists describe this mode of adaptation?
    a. Pastoralism
    b. Horticulture
    c. Intensive agriculture

15. Which of the following is <u>NOT</u> a feature of postindustrialism?
    a. Explosive population growth
    b. Decreased resource consumption
    c. Focus away from food, toward technology and service

16. In the 19th century, many believed that <u>all cultures went through the same stages of development</u>. Western society was viewed as the peak of civilization. What is this discredited theory called?
    a. Historical particularism
    b. Unilineal evolution
    c. Biological Eugenics

17. Franz Boas, the father of Modern Anthropology, stated that cultural development does not occur along one universal scale. Instead, <u>differences are the result of each group's unique history</u>. This theory is referred to as:
    a. Historical particularism
    b. Unilineal evolution
    c. Biological Eugenics

18. One of the key factors in the horrific failure of Franklin's expedition was the view of Inuit culture as inferior. This led to dismissal of local knowledge and inability to adapt to the environment. <u>Judging another culture through your own cultural lens</u> is referred to as:
    a. Cultural relativity
    b. Ethnocentricity
    c. Cultural ethnorelativity

19. Artifacts recovered by the McClintock Expedition included peculiar items, such as button polish and books. Inuit technology, such as lightweight sleds and weapons for hunting large game, were noticeably absent. What does this array of supplies suggest about Franklin's Expedition?
    a. They did not expect to leave the ships and were unequipped for the environment
    b. Beliefs that the Inuits were inferior people led to dismissal of Inuit knowledge
    c. All of the above

20. Multiple subfields of anthropology have been involved in the Franklin mystery. Which subfield of anthropology does Dr. Owen Beattie's team represent?
    a. Arctic archaeology
    b. Forensic anthropology
    c. Cultural anthropology

CHAPTER II: THE CASE OF FRANKLIN'S LOST EXPEDITION

1.	True	11.	C
2.	False	12.	A
3.	False	13.	A
4.	False	14.	C
5.	True	15.	B
6.	A	16.	B
7.	B	17.	A
8.	B	18.	B
9.	C	19.	C
10.	A	20.	B

CHAPTER III

WATER, WATER, EVERYWHERE

Culture, Economics, and Poverty in the Land of Plenty

"The upper class: keeps all of the money, pays none of the taxes.

The middle class: pays all of the taxes, does all of the work.

The poor are there just to scare the shit out of the middle class."

– George Carlin, Jammin' in New York (1992)

When George Carlin delivered this scathing indictment of America's economic class system, he was already a comedy legend. Although success had placed him within the ranks of the wealthy, his views stemmed from working class roots. Carlin's vitriol was fueled by mistrust towards the upper class, whom he saw as blind to the plight of the poor. He summarized this perspective by adding, ". . . ever notice there's no war on homelessness . . . You know why? There's no money in that problem . . . Nobody stands to get rich off of that problem. You could find a solution to homelessness, where the corporate swine and the politicians could steal a couple million dollars each, you'd see the streets of America begin to clear up pretty god damn quick . . .". While you may not agree with Carlin's assessment, it illustrates the relationship between culture and economics that is central to this chapter.

The focus of this chapter is **socioeconomics**, the relationship between culture, social structure, and economics. Culture shapes your belief about the causes of poverty, which informs how you think it can be resolved. For example, if you feel that complacency and welfare dependence is rampant among America's poor. You are more likely to support measures you believe will motivate impoverished people to seek employment. You are less likely to support increased funding for social assistance, as this would be viewed as encouraging welfare dependence. Persistent poverty in the US will serve as the centerpiece of our socioeconomic examination. The key question is not how people become poor in the first place, but why it is so difficult to escape poverty in one of the world's wealthiest nations.

The key elements of ongoing economic hardship will be assessed in four parts. **Part One, "Wife-swapping and Wealth"**, provides a general explanation of how modes of adaptation give rise to cultural beliefs about economic inequality.

Part Two, "They Eat Rats", applies these principles to past views of poverty in the US. This section analyzes the historical foundation and consequences of these traditional cultural beliefs. **Part Three, "Familiar Faces"**, introduces the new face of poverty in America. Theories highlighting various causes of persistent poverty are presented in **Part Four, "How to Build a Poorhouse"**. These theories offer various ways of looking at the roots of ongoing economic hardship.

PART I: WIFE-SWAPPING & WEALTH

Modes of Adaptation Shape Economic Views

Economic systems are means of regulating access to key resources; such as food, shelter, and education. Determining who should have access to which resources and how much is imperative to group survival. Decisions about resource distribution are based on cultural beliefs. Those who adhere to the group's cultural norms and values are identified as insiders, thus deserving of access to resources. Deviation from these cultural parameters can hinder access by harming in-group status or at worst, being ejected from the group and labeled an "outsider." This is exemplified by the stereotype of poor people as lazy. Deviating from mainstream cultural values (*i.e. hard work*) casts the poor as undeserving of access, which decreases support for social assistance programs. This sentiment emerges in welfare reform debates, with statements such as, "My hard-earned money shouldn't be used to support someone who doesn't want to work." **Cultural beliefs about the causes of economic hardship determine the actions taken to alleviate it.**

Cultural views of poverty are rooted in our modes of adaptation[1], or how groups create and/or acquire resources (*e.g. food, shelter, income*). These systems of survival produce varying amounts of resources. Hunting and gathering provides enough food to sustain the group, but little to no surplus. Industrialism, which focuses on manufacturing, yields a large amount of excess food. **The amount of surplus generated influences social structure** (*e.g. egalitarian, hierarchical*).

When there is little to no surplus, resources must be distributed equally in order for the group to survive. Large amounts of surplus require more management, which means that some individuals will have more control over how resources are distributed than others. This leads to centralization of power and social hierarchy, inevitably creating economic inequality. **Culture shapes our interpretations of socioeconomic inequality.**

The indigenous[2] Canela people of Brazil provide a model of how modes of adaptation shape cultural values and views of equality. This Amazonian group traditionally relies on a combination of hunting, gathering, and horticulture. These modes of adaptation produce very little surplus and equal sharing of resources is crucial to survival. This is sometimes accomplished through ceremonies requiring contributions of meat acquired from the day's hunting activities to a single pool that is later redistributed to all group members. A member who refuses to contribute or hoards meat is seen as a threat to the group's well-being and risks becoming an outcast. Pooling resources prevents the accumulation of wealth, which gives rise to a relatively egalitarian social structure. Subsequently, traditional Canela culture emphasizes the importance of community over individual. This cultural value is reflected in other areas of Canela life, such as festivals in which tribal members engage in group, sequential, and extramarital sex. Members who become possessive of their spouses and try to stop them from having sex with others during these celebrations are viewed poorly. Since the egalitarian social structure doesn't necessitate the guarding of wealth or property from other group members, the benefits of spousal sharing outweighs potential risks.[3] Participation reinforces the virtue of placing community cohesion over personal needs.

When modes of adaptation produce scarce surplus, upholding egalitarian values is key to the group's survival. One individual or family retaining a significantly larger portion of resources deviates from cultural norms and

---

[1] Modes of adaptation are detailed further in Chapter 2; Part II: *The World of Sir John Franklin*; Section B: *Of Savages and Men.*

[2] **Indigenous**—People occupying an area prior to the establishment of the State (e.g. Native Americans in the US).

[3] Middletone, DeWight R. *The Challenge of Human Diversity: Mirrors, Bridges, and Chasms.* 3rd Ed. Illinois: Waveland Press, 2011. 96. Print.

values. This would be interpreted negatively, likely harming social status and possibly resulting in rejection from the group. **Modes of adaptation give rise to economic systems, which produce and are reinforced by cultural beliefs.**

PART II: THEY EAT RATS

Past Views of Poverty and the American Dream

"New Yorkers say things like, 'They'll eat you down there. They eat rats. You'll be killed,'" recalled Marc Singer of the warnings he'd received when he decided to leave the modeling world to live among the city's mysterious "mole people."[4] Singer's decision to abandon his modeling career and Manhattan loft resulted in *Dark Days*, a riveting documentary of a the mysterious "mole people." [5] Beneath the lavish wealth of Manhattan, hundreds of makeshift shelters pepper the subway tunnels. Even more surprising than the existence of these bizarre villages were the features found inside some of the houses, such as electricity and running water. In 2007, Matthew O'Brien published his experiences with the population occupying the scorpion-laden flood tunnels below the iconic Las Vegas strip.[6] Works like those of Singer and O'Brien humanized the mysterious mole people by revealing common elements within their Otherness. For example, Singer's *Dark Days* included scenes in which characters discussed relatable topics such as parenting and pets. These works marked a cultural turning point in America regarding the poor, as the characters featured were incohesive with traditional stereotypes.

The startling proximity of extreme poverty and wealth symbolizes one of the most frustrating quandaries of the modern world: **Why does poverty persist in post-industrial societies?** It is important to note the word "persistent" in this discussion of poverty. While infinite events can thrust anyone into economic hardship, the difficulty of escaping or recovering from poverty is far more baffling. Possible answers to this daunting question reside in the intersection of culture and economics. Traditionally, introductory textbooks illustrate this concept using examples of economic systems as they arise in various cultures. While this is an excellent way of demonstrating the origins of cultural variety, this text will focus on cultural interpretations of economic disparity in the United States.

Modern stereotypes of the poor as lazy, uneducated, and morally deficient are an American tradition. By this, I mean that they were inherited by the country's earliest generations. In order to comprehend views of poverty today, it is necessary to examine its cultural origins. In the 19th century, American industrialization gave rise to immense surplus and a distinct hierarchy of socioeconomic classes.

Impoverished children of the underclass toiled in dangerous factories as the elite Victorian upper class attended extravagant galas. Cultural interpretations of these disparities were shaped by the Protestant values of the nation's founding fathers. Protestantism dictates that hard work, persistence, and prudence demonstrate dedication to Christianity. German sociologist Max Weber theorized that this ideological framework influenced modern forms of capitalism.[7] If characteristics of the "Protestant work ethic" are an indicator of moral righteousness, then wealth is framed as a reward for virtue. Subsequently, poverty is perceived as evidence of lacking moral fiber. The principle that hard work is rewarded by success relies on

---

[4] Sandhu, Sukhdev. "Dark Days: Going Underground with New York's Tunnel Dwellers." *The Guardian*. 26 Jan. 2014. Web. 11 Apr. 2015.

[5] *Dark Days*. Dir. M. Singer. Wide Angle Pictures and Palm Pictures. 2000. Film.

[6] O'Brien, Matthew. *Beneath the Neon: Life and Death in the Tunnels of Las Vegas*. Las Vegas: Huntington Press, 2007. Print.

[7] Weber, Max. *The Protestant Ethic and the Spirit of Capitalism*. New York: Scribner, 1958. Print.

the presupposition that poverty is the penalty for moral failure. This ideology was reflected in the popularity of Horatio Alger's rags-to-riches stories. Alger's protagonists consistently triumphed over poverty through diligence and determination. Such stories captured the idealistic expectation of success embedded in American culture. American author William Dean Howells is alleged to have stated, "What the American public wants is a tragedy with a happy ending. . . [*this attitude*] is true of the whole American attitude toward life."[8] His implication being that Americans maintain a steadfast belief in the ability to overcome any circumstance, including abject poverty. For some, economic success validated the American dream. Based on this belief, the affluent sought means of clearing up the patches of poverty that blemished the landscape.

During the 1900s, the **Biological Theory** proposed that poverty was determined at birth by inherited traits. Behaviors associated with poverty, such as promiscuity and criminality, were viewed as inherited genetic deficiencies. The obvious flaw in this theory being that it discounts the ability of humans to learn and ignores the role of larger societal factors. This assumption was bolstered by the prevalence of "inferior" racial and ethnic groups in slums. Based on this belief, eradicating poverty could be accomplished by keeping the poor from reproducing. This approach, championed by scientists and affluent members of society, prompted the eugenics movement. **Eugenics** is controlling reproduction to increase desirable characteristics in upcoming generations. As a result, over 80,000 Americans were sterilized and castrated, most of whom were of the impoverished classes.[9] This dark period in US history demonstrates the power that cultural beliefs have on the lives of those around us.

PART III: FAMILIAR FACES

American Poverty in the Present Day

In August 2014, 32 year-old Maria Fernandes parked her 2001 Kia Sportage in a convenience store lot in New Jersey. Maria had been trying to make ends meet by working at multiple Dunkin' Donuts locations. Already in uniform, she decided to take a nap before heading into her next shift. As she drifted into slumber, she was unaware that the gas can she kept in her car had leaked. When New Jersey police discovered Maria, she was already dead.

Headlines such as, "Dunkin' Donuts Worker's Death Reveals the True Cost of Our Low-Wage, Part-Time Economy",[10] flooded media outlets. Accounts of hard- working Americans trapped in poverty multiplied, contradicting the stereotype of the lazy, deviant poor. Some dismissed stories of struggling minimum wage workers as a consequence of limited ambitions, stating that the working poor could have pursued educations to attain better paying jobs. This response echoed the idealism of the Horatio Alger era, as well as traditional views of poverty as a consequence of moral shortcomings. However, this foundation of the American dream was also on shaky ground as faces of the highly educated were gaining attention among the poor.

In 2013, The Pittsburgh Post-Gazette published an op-ed titled, "Death of an Adjunct".[11] Margaret Mary Vojtko, an adjunct French professor of 25 years at Duquesne University, spent her final days in destitution and near homelessness.

---

[8] Wharton, Edith. French Ways and Their Meaning. London: D. Appleton and Company, 1919. Print.

[9] Black, Edwin. *War Against the Weak: Eugenics and America's Campaign to Create a Master Race.* New York: Thunder's Mouth Press, 2004. Print.

[10] Berman, Jillian. "Dunkin' Donuts Worker's Death Reveals the True Cost of Our Low-Wage, Part-Time Economy." *The Huffington Post.* 29 Aug. 2014. Web. 4 Apr. 2015.

[11] Kovalik, Daniel. "Death of an Adjunct." *Pittsburgh Post-Gazette.* N.p. 18 Sep. 2013. Web.1 Mar. 2015.

Vojtko's tragic situation contradicted the stereotype of professor positions as cushy and lucrative. The case brought attention to the little-known struggles of part-time adjunct professors. While most of the public was unaware of the difference between full-time and part-time professors, adjuncts comprise approximately 76% of University faculty. These are instructors with advanced degrees, paid on a semester-to-semester contract basis. Without eligibility to apply for tenure, this means that adjunct instructors lack job security and 75% receive no benefits. Most receive $2700 per three-credit course, with the median salary falling at approximately $22,041 a year.[12] When Forbes listed "University Professor" as the least stressful job of 2013, it sparked considerable backlash from adjunct professors. On Twitter, #realforbesprofessors yielded snarky comments such as, "As an adjunct professor, I never worry about healthcare – the student health center has free bandaids and condoms - @pseudoknot". Accounts of adjuncts, many with PhDs, relying on government assistance and juggling multiple low-wage jobs became fixtures in the socioeconomic landscape.

Stories like those of Maria Fernandes and Margaret Mary Vojtko called attention to an oft-overlooked segment of society. "**The working poor**" refers to people who work at least 27 weeks out of the year, yet remain below the poverty line. The **poverty line** is the minimum income deemed adequate to care for a household according to the government (**Fig 1**). Census statistics on poverty report those living BELOW the poverty line, but those above this line are often faced with the same struggles. For perspective, consider the 2014 poverty line for a family of four ($23,850/yr.). For a single person living in a low priced city, this salary can be challenging to manage. Additionally, this calculation does not include expenses for extenuating circumstances such as vehicular repairs or health emergencies. Cultural beliefs and economic systems serve to reinforce one another.

POVERTY IN THE U.S.
Poverty line: Min. level of income adequate to care for a household

2014 POVERTY GUIDELINES FOR THE 48 CONTIGUOUS STATES AND THE DISTRICT OF COLUMBIA

Persons in family/household	Poverty guideline
1	$11,670
2	15,730
3	19,790
4	23,850
5	27,910
6	31,970
7	36,030
8	40,090
For families/households with more than 8 persons, add $4,060 for each additional person.	

Fig. 1: 2014 Poverty Guidelines[13]

[12]"The Just-in-Time Professor." House Committee on Education and the Workforce Democratic Staff. U.S. House of Representatives. January 2014.
[13]"2014 Federal Poverty Guidelines." *Office of the Assistant Secretary for Planning and Evaluation, HHS.* U.S. Department of Health and Human Services, 22 Jan. 2014. Web. 3 Mar. 2015.

Subsequently, changes in resource availability affect economic systems and result in cultural shifts. For example, the Canela of Brazil traditionally relied on modes of adaptation providing very little surplus. As a result, a great of emphasis was placed on communal sharing. In recent years, increased contact with nearby industrialized cities has allowed individuals to acquire and accumulate resources without relying on other group members. Thus, there is a decreased need for communal sharing and greater potential for social inequality, as some members will own significantly more property than others. Traditions promoting communalism have become virtually non-existent among the younger generations. Among the Canela, the shift in resources has resulted in a change in cultural values.

In post-industrial America, resource availability was dramatically affected by economic recessions and massive job loss. As economic hardship stretched resources beyond their limits, middle and upper class families joined the ranks of the poor. In 2013, the Census Bureau reported 45 million people, or approximately 14.5% of the US population, were living below the poverty line.[14] The shock of falling into poverty was further amplified by the horror of being unable to escape it. Scores of Americans found themselves homeless, a possibility that most had never imagined. The U.S. Department of Housing and Urban Development reported that approximately 578, 424 people were homeless on any given night in January 2014. Former members of the middle and upper classes began to occupy underground communities and "tent cities." Being trapped in a socioeconomic nightmare traditionally reserved for the morally bankrupt forced many to reimagine the American dream.

PART IV: HOW TO BUILD A POORHOUSE

Theories of Persistent Poverty

Evaluating causes of persistent poverty can reveal barriers to escaping its clutches. In this section, we will discuss **five theories of persistent poverty**. Keep in mind that the complexity of socioeconomic status cannot be explained by a single factor. Each theory presents a different interpretation of which factors are most significant to sustaining poverty. Perceptions of which factors are strongest influence the solutions that you choose to support or resist.

A. CULTURE OF POVERTY

Anthropologist Oscar Lewis coined the term "culture of poverty" in his 1961 ethnography, *The Children of Sanchez: Autobiography of a Mexican Family*.[15] The book followed the lives of Jesus Sanchez and his four adult children as told from their perspectives. Lewis identified approximately fifty behavioral patterns and traditions comprising the "culture of poverty." According to Lewis, these systems developed in response to the conditions of abject poverty.

Additionally, many behaviors that were adaptive for impoverished conditions were counterproductive to social mobility. Lewis' concept has become a fixture of discussions regarding poverty in the US. Although controversial, the culture of poverty theory has been refurbished and reintroduced in the new socioeconomic landscape.

---

[14]U.S. Department of Commerce. United States Census Bureau. *Income, Poverty and Health Insurance Coverage in the U.S.: 2013. Newsroom.* United States Census Bureau, 16 Sept. 2014. Web. 2 Mar. 2015.

[15]Lewis, Oscar. *The Children of Sanchez: An Autobiography of a Mexican Family.* New York: Random House, 1961.

In 1965, an in-house communication from the Department of Labor to the Presidential administration titled "The Negro Family: The Case for National Action" was leaked to the press. The piece, commonly referred to as "the Moynihan report", in reference to its author, was intended to provide a basis for anti-poverty programs in the African American population. According to the Moynihan report, slavery and ongoing discrimination trapped African American families in a "tangle of pathology". Symptoms of this pathology were, among others: a high rate of single mothers, absentee fathers, and welfare dependency. These cultural characteristics, the report proposed, created volatility within African American families. **Moynihan concluded that chronic instability of African American family units was a major cause of the community's disproportionate poverty.** Based on these conclusions, Moynihan urged the government to develop programs aimed at restructuring African American families. While some agreed with his sentiment, others felt his assumptions were grounded in the racist assumption that African Americans lacked morality. Controversy erupted as critics accused Moynihan of essentially blaming African Americans for their own poverty.[16] Public backlash rendered any mention of the culture of poverty taboo for nearly forty years.

On May 13, 2010, academics and policymakers met in Washington, D.C. for a Congressional briefing titled, "Reconsidering Culture and Poverty". Interest in the role of culture in persistent poverty has been resurrected, but without the vehement public response. Like the traditional version, the revised theory views behaviors linked to the culture of poverty as an obstacle to socioeconomic advancement. **Unlike the traditional version, the revised culture of poverty includes the insider's perspective on what motivates their behaviors.** Application of this relativistic framework has been crucial to avoiding the pitfalls of the Moynihan report. Evaluating behaviors within the culture of poverty as choices can reveal intentions that may redefine stereotypes of the poor. Sociologists Kathryn Edin and Maria Kefalas surprised many with conclusions drawn from interviews with 162 low-income single mothers in Philadelphia, Pennsylvania. Contrary to traditional stereotypes, the women did not choose to remain single because they didn't value marriage. They opted to remain single because of their belief in its importance and didn't believe that their partners were "marriage material."[17] This data brought some policymakers to the realization that programs promoting marriage were fruitless without improved circumstances to yield more eligible partners. The revised theory provides valuable insight into behavioral patterns contributing to persistent poverty. Understanding the meaning and cause of these actions can lead to more effective policies to resolve the issue.

The current or revised view of the culture of poverty views traits as adaptive for the impoverished environment. For example, it is necessary for people living in poor, urban areas to project an air of toughness. Mannerisms and speech patterns are shaped to fit the parameters of these cultural norms. In this environment, these behaviors demonstrate insider status and reduce the possibility of being targeted. However, the same demeanor may be misinterpreted as aloof or aggressive in more stable environments. This does not discount the ability of people to learn and adjust, but it takes time for cultural behaviors to be integrated into the natural repertoire. In the case of the poor, time required to acquire these skills may not be an available option. Consider how much of your daily demeanor occurs automatically, such as physical distance and eye contact made during conversation. When placed within a new cultural context, these "natural" behaviors can lead to you unwittingly offend others, perhaps losing opportunities that you didn't even know existed.

---

[16] Ryan, William. *Blaming the Victim*. New York: Pantheon Books, 1971. Print.

[17] Edin, Kathryn and Maria Kefalas. *Promises I Can Keep: Why Poor Women Put Motherhood before Marriage*. Berkeley: University of California Press, 2005.

B. CULTURAL CAPITAL

Cultural capital is fluency in the culture of the elite. This includes knowledge needed to successfully navigate and benefit from opportunities in affluent environments.[18] In a sense, cultural capital and the culture of poverty are two sides of one coin. The culture of poverty examines behaviors resulting from the unstable, impoverished environment. Cultural capital refers to behaviors and skills acquired from life among the middle and upper classes. Engagement and familiarity with cultural traditions signals your status in relation to a group. Culture is a rapid way to identify an "outsider", a label that negatively affects your access to resources. Cues such as body language and manner of speaking shape how others perceive you, sometimes in ways that they are unaware of. These signals affect the relationships that can open, close, or create doors of opportunity.

Sociologist Annette Lareau observed 88 African American and Caucasian families from a variety of economic levels. Her findings revealed that differences in parenting styles were dictated by economics more than race. For example, parents of the lower and middle classes responded differently when children expressed interest in an activity. Lower class parents perceived it as personality trait, as in, "Oh, Katie just likes to dance." These parents offered informal encouragement and allowed children to pursue interests spontaneously with little interference, a process Lareau referred to as "**natural growth.**" When middle class parents identified an interest, they employed "**concerted cultivation.**" These parents invested resources into "cultivating" or guiding the child's interest through scheduled activities. Each parenting style yielded different advantages for the children. Lareau found that working class kids had tighter emotional networks, while middle class also had a looser sense of community but larger networks. Concerted cultivation provided middle class children two advantages later in life. First, this form of encouragement instilled in them sense of **entitlement**, or belief in their right to pursue interests. Second, familiarization with institutionalized settings (ex. classes) provided children with **cultural capital**. Engagement in structured settings allowed the children to learn how to successfully advocate for themselves. Later in life, they are better prepared to negotiate and even bend rules to suit their needs. They are better prepared to create opportunities for themselves in the institutional settings common to the professional world.

Cultural capital can be acquired, but not instantaneously. Programs for learning professionalism can be beneficial for individuals coming from impoverished environments. One example of this is a summer program aimed at preparing students from underprivileged backgrounds for their first semester of college. Along with teaching the students how to manage their time and ultimately, transition into the environment of higher education, students also learn how to appropriately interact with instructors. Many students are the first in their families to navigate the professional environment and lack the cultural capital to successfully operate within the norms. The result is that, like being a foreigner who unfamiliar with local customs, students may unwittingly present themselves in a negative manner. One of the most difficult habits for many to change is addressing the instructor as "Professor/Doctor", as opposed to "Mr./Ms./Mrs.". Although some instructors express apathy toward the title used by students, initial use of the title provides the subtle, positive indicator of professionalism.

C. SOCIAL STRUCTURAL THEORY

This theory states that formal structures sustain poverty through a lack of opportunities. Formal structures are defined as overarching systems, such as education or employment, that limit the socioeconomic mobility

---

[18] Bourdieu, Pierre. "The forms of capital." *Handbook of Theory and Research for the Sociology of Education.* Ed. J. Richardson. New York, Greenwood: 1986. 241–258. Print.

of the poor. In contrast to the culture of poverty theory's bottom-up perspective, social structural theory takes a decisive top-down approach. For example, Sociologist William Julius Wilson pointed to inadequate social institutions as major contributors to concentrated poverty in New Orleans neighborhoods devastated by Hurricane Katrina in 2005. According to Wilson, lack of jobs, inadequate educational systems, and institutionalized discrimination gave rise to the poverty that rendered thousands unable to evacuate prior to the storm.[19] Although problems <u>within</u> each institution are identifiable, the dynamic relationship between <u>systems</u> complicates the search for solutions.

The link between education and employment renders these systems sensitive to one others flaws and fluctuations. Understaffed, poorly equipped schools produce students who are at a disadvantage when competing for admission to college or applying for jobs. However, resolving this issue is not as simple as improving the school systems. In 2012, *The New York Times* documented the complexities of problem-solving within single institutions. The article presented a surprising reason for the failure of literacy programs in the hills of Eastern Kentucky.[20] In the scenic hills of Appalachia, some of the nation's poorest counties have come to rely on government assistance for basic survival. Anti-poverty programs identified staggering illiteracy rates as a factor limiting employment and trapping many in poverty. Well-intentioned programs aimed at improving literacy became available for students, a seemingly logical solution. So many were stunned when parents quickly removed their children from the programs. An overlooked detail was that many families were receiving nearly $700 per month in Supplemental Security Income (SSI) for each child diagnosed with a disability. Parents feared that improved academic performance would no longer qualify them as learning disabled, leading to a loss of the hefty SSI checks the families relied on. Advocacy groups continue trying to promote literacy using alternative routes, such as home visits. The Eastern Kentucky case provides an example of structural limitations (i.e. education, employment) contributing to persistent employment, as well as the difficulties of effectively resolving them.

D. FUNCTIONALIST APPROACH

This theory states that the poverty will be sustained as long as the poor fulfill positive societal functions for the middle and upper classes. If society is imagined as an ecosystem, then the poor are similar to the bacteria vital for the recycling and decomposition of waste. These functions do not mean that poverty SHOULD or MUST exist, but that it affects willingness of the affluent to aid the poor—since they benefit from their existence. Based on this theory, measures to truly eradicate or combat poverty will only occur when its effects begin to affect the non- poor. Supporters of this theory might point to the surge of interest in poverty since the recession began to pull the middle class into inescapable poverty.

Sociologist Herbert Gans identified thirteen functions of the poor for the non poor.[21] For our purposes, we will focus on three aspects of these functions:

1. **Turning Trash into Treasure**

    The poor take on jobs and purchase products deemed undesirable to the non-poor. Undesirable "dirty work" often involves intense physical labor, dangerous conditions, and/or low wages. Low incomes also necessitate saving by purchasing used items, such as clothing and cars, which prolongs the usefulness of products.

---

[19] Wilson, William Julius. "Being Poor, Black, and American: The Impact of Political, Economic, and Cultural Forces." *American Educator* (Spring 2011): 10–23. Print.

[20] Kristof, Nicholas. "Profiting From a Child's Illiteracy." *The New York Times*. 9 Dec. 2012: SR1. Print.

[21] Gans, Herbert. "The Uses of Poverty: The Poor Pay All." *Social Policy* (July/August 1971): 20–24. Print.

2. **Creating Jobs for the Non-Poor**

   Impoverished communities generate employment for fields providing for the poor, such as social services. Additionally, they sustain jobs in systems to shield the rest of society from them, such as police and correctional officers.

3. **Social Deviants and Cultural Heroes**

   The poor are used to represent both ends of the societal spectrum for the non-poor, from dangerous criminals to the dignified downtrodden. If the intention is to reinforce cultural norms, then the poor are presented as examples of deviance and immoral behavior. While general criminality among the underclass has not been proven to exist at a higher rate than the non-poor, the poor are more likely to be arrested and penalized more harshly. The resulting high rate of the poor among the prison population upholds this stereotype.

   On the other end of the spectrum, the poor can also be envisioned as cultural heroes. This is evident in common tropes, such as the kind-hearted prostitute or the sagacious hobo. The affluent also appropriate cultural artifacts from the downtrodden, evidenced by the popularity of rock and jazz music. Politicians often promote, sometimes exaggerate, their own economic struggles. Most recently, "hipster" fashion has popularized wearing ironically outdated clothing. The trend has prompted scores of middle and upper class youth to raid secondhand stores for well- worn items. Adoption of an intentionally impoverished aesthetic by the affluent, referred to in the media as the "poorgeoisie"[22] has spawned websites challenging visitors to differentiate photos of hipsters from those of the homeless.

   Representations of the poor utilized by the affluent are maintained by the poor's lack of influence to counteract these perceptions.

According to Gans, efforts to resolve poverty effectively are most likely to occur under one or both of the following conditions:

1. **The dysfunction of poverty outweighs its function:**

   When the problems of poverty begin to significantly affect the affluent, who have the resources to address income inequality, then the issue will be effectively approached. For example, imagine that the cost of addressing crime (ex. patrols, security cameras) in an impoverished neighborhood EXCEEDS the income generated by jobs in the criminal justice sector (ex. police, correctional officers). If this happens, it is more cost-effective to identify and address larger factors that might be leading to crime, such as joblessness.

2. **The poor develop a means to exert power or influence:**

   This condition states that poverty can be resolved if the poor can access resources without needing to rely on the affluent. It is important to note that Gans' piece was published in 1971, prior to the ubiquity of the Internet. The online world has the potential to provide a truly level playing field for the first time in human history.

   The ability to congregate and exchange ideas online has given rise to groups like Anonymous, a loosely organized network of individuals from all socioeconomic strata. Free from traditional restrictions, such as travel expenses or connections to the affluent, the digital landscape allows the poor to influence systems of power.

---

[22] **Poorgeoisie**—Combination of "poor" and "bourgeoisie," the latter term refers to the middle and upper classes.

Understanding how culture shapes views of inequality will give you with the ability to evaluate the issue from multiple vantage points. Being able to see from someone else's perspective, even if you don't agree with them, allows you to foresee potential obstacles to implementing various solutions. For example, you might propose allocating tax funds to provide vocational training for the homeless. If taxpayers view homelessness as a result of moral deficiency, such as unwillingness to work or criminality, then they are unlikely to support this measure. Failure to adhere to cultural standards marks someone as an outsider, rendering them ineligible (or in this case, undeserving) for resources. Based on this, you may either decide on a different strategy or alter the way in which the free vocational training is presented. **Cultural interpretations of economic status have a direct and significant impact on approaches to poverty.**

PRACTICE EXAM QUESTIONS
CHAPTER III: WATER, WATER EVERYWHERE

T F 1. <u>Economic systems</u> are means of managing resources, primarily through regulating access.

T F 2. During the 1900s, the <u>Culture of Poverty</u> theory was used to support the eugenics movement.

T F 3. Theories of poverty are primarily focused on <u>how people become poor in the first place</u>.

T F 4. The <u>poverty line</u> is defined as the minimum income deemed adequate to care for a household by the government.

T F 5. Behaviors developed as an adaptation to an unstable, impoverished environment are referred to as <u>cultural capital</u>.

6. In 2012, *The Guardian*'s photograph of three women at New York Fashion Week fueled national debates. Some felt that the image was symbolic of class inequality in the United States. What did the image appear to portray?

   a. Two women in high-end clothing mocking a woman wearing a fast food uniform

   b. A famous fashion designer hiring three homeless women as models

   c. Upper-class women obliviously or indifferently posing beside a homeless man

7. Marc Singer's film and Matthew O'Brien's book document a specific segment of America's homeless population. What do their subjects have in common?

   a. They live in makeshift shelters in the tunnels beneath bustling, prosperous cities

   b. All of their subjects dropped out of high school or college

   c. They are all addicted to prescription painkillers

8. How do traditional American beliefs about poverty reflect Protestant beliefs?

   a. It is believed that only Christians can become truly wealthy

   b. Wealth is attributed to hard work; poverty is attributed to laziness

   c. Poverty is viewed as a sign of virtue and spiritual righteousness

9. During the 1900s, the Biological Theory led many scientists and affluent members of society to support the eugenics movement. What was this movement?

   a. Food programs to eliminate the malnutrition causing genetic deficiencies

   b. Fines placed on lower-income families for having more than one child

   c. Controlling reproduction to increase desirable traits in upcoming generations

10. How did Maria Fernandes's story conflict with stereotypes of the American poor?

   a. She had multiple jobs; conflicted with the stereotype of the poor as lazy

   b. She was a professor; conflicted with the stereotype of the poor as uneducated

   c. She was a youth pastor; conflicted with the stereotype of the poor as amoral

11. How did Margaret Mary Vojtko's story conflict with stereotypes of the American poor?

   a. She had multiple jobs; conflicted with the stereotype of the poor as lazy

   b. She was a professor; conflicted with the stereotype of the poor as uneducated

   c. She was a youth pastor; conflicted with the stereotype of the poor as amoral

12. Kayla is a single woman working over 27 weeks per year as a part-time chemistry professor. Her annual income is around $9,500/year, placing her below the poverty line for a single person. Which term describes Kayla's economic status?
    a. Functionally impoverished
    b. Breaking bank
    c. The working poor

13. In the ethnography *The Children of Sanchez: Autobiography of a Mexican Family*, which term did anthropologist Oscar Lewis coin to describe the behavioral patterns and traditions he observed?
    a. The working poor
    b. Culture of poverty
    c. Functionalist poverty

14. The "Moynihan Report" concluded that chronic instability of African American family units was a major cause of the community's disproportionate poverty. What was the primary criticism of the report?
    a. It focused solely on African Americans and did not offer solutions for rising poverty in the Hispanic community
    b. The report lacked interview and statistical data
    c. It implied lack of morality among African Americans and blamed them for their own poverty

15. The revised Culture of Poverty theory evaluates behaviors as choices, a view that encourages researchers to investigate insider perspectives and motives. One example of this was regarding the high rate of single mothers in poor communities. What did sociologists Kathryn Edin and Maria Kefalas find?
    a. Single mothers did not value marriage
    b. The poor did not want to spend money on marriage licenses
    c. Single mothers placed high value on marriage and did not see their partners as "marriage material"

16. Sociologist Annette Lareau found that parenting styles differed greatly between economic classes. Which strategies did the lower- and middle-class parents employ when their children expressed interests?
    a. Lower = "natural growth"; Middle = "concerted cultivation"
    b. Lower = "concerted cultivation"; Middle = "natural growth"
    c. Lower = "entitlement"; Middle = "concerted cultivation"

17. Sociologist William Julius Wilson pointed to inadequate social institutions, such as lack of jobs, as a major contributor to the concentrated poverty that prevented many from evacuating New Orleans prior to Hurricane Katrina in 2005. Which theory does this support?
    a. Functionalist Theory
    b. Culture of Poverty Theory
    c. Social Structural Theory

18. Social Structural Theory of Poverty states that lack of opportunities, such as jobs, sustains poverty. How did lack of employment lead to the failure of literacy programs in Eastern Kentucky?
    a. Children were dropping out to work; programs were only available to students
    b. Parents feared that children with improved grades would no longer be eligible for SSI, so removed children from literacy programs
    c. Parents were unable to afford basic supplies required by literacy programs

19. According to Functionalist Theory, poverty is sustained as long as the poor fulfill positive societal functions for the middle and upper class. Which function is served by crime and unemployment among the poor?
    a. Turning trash into treasure
    b. Creating jobs for the nonpoor
    c. Being reimagined as cultural heroes

20. According to sociologist Herbert Gans, one of two conditions must occur before poverty can effectively be resolved. Which of these conditions does the online hacktivist collective, Anonymous, demonstrate?
    a. The dysfunction of poverty outweighs its function
    b. The poor learn to capitalize on their image as cultural heroes
    c. The poor develop a means to exert power or influence

CHAPTER III: WATER, WATER EVERYWHERE

1.	True	11.	B
2.	False	12.	C
3.	False	13.	B
4.	True	14.	C
5.	False	15.	C
6.	C	16.	A
7.	A	17.	C
8.	B	18.	B
9.	C	19.	B
10.	A	20.	C

CHAPTER IV

THE FILMMAKER'S DAUGHTER

Cultural Constructions of Kinship and Marriage

"The heart wants what it wants. There's no logic to those things.

You meet someone and you fall in love and that's that."

– Woody Allen[1]

On January 3, 1992, a stack of photographs shattered a family and scandalized the American public. At this time, filmmaker Woody Allen and actress Mia Farrow had been together for over a decade. Eccentric in opposite ways, the duration of their relationship surprised many. Allen was an impish playboy, while family-centric Farrow entered the relationship with an entourage of seven biological and adopted children. To the delight of the public, the pair endured by crafting a relationship as unconventional as their personalities. They never wed and maintained separated homes in New York City, even while sharing custody of three children. But it was the most unusual aspect of their relationship that would bring their romance to a shocking, bitter end. On this day, Allen was on set directing his latest film when he received a call from Farrow's attorney.[2] While in Allen's home, Farrow had made a devastating discovery. Beneath a tissue box, Farrow found six photos of a nude woman posed provocatively with her legs spread. The graphic portraits revealed that not only was Allen having an affair, but also that it was with Farrow's adopted daughter, Soon-Yi.

Conflicting interpretations of the affair dominated headlines and became comedic fodder. Some painted 56-year-old Allen as a lecher preying on an innocent Soon-Yi, 35 years his junior. Others portrayed Soon-Yi as a stereotypical dragon-lady or shrewd seductress. Central to many discussions was whether or not it was incestuous. Incest is defined as sexual relations between individuals of inappropriately close relation. However, the complexity of Farrow and Allen's union made the boundaries of relatedness unclear. Questions remained even after Woody Allen and Soon-Yi wed in 1997. At the time of this writing, they have been married for over 20 years and are raising two adopted daughters. Professionally, Allen has maintained his place in the pantheon of iconic filmmakers. However, the scandal left an indelible mark on public perception of his personal life.

Cultural perceptions have the power to define our actions as virtuous or villainous. The controversy surrounding Woody and Soon-Yi was fueled by differing opinions of their relatedness. Cultural constructions of kinship yielded wildly contrasting views of their relationship as repulsively incestuous or a run-of-the-mill Hollywood affair. In this chapter, we will explore the two most powerful organizing forces in every society: kinship and marriage. Each system is examined in its own section, with Part I dedicated to kinship and Part II focused on marriage. However, they have been paired in this chapter because, as will become apparent, they are inextricably intertwined.

---

[1] Isaacson, Walter. "The Heart Wants What it Wants." TIME Magazine. 24 June 2001. Web. 1 June 2015.
[2] Hainey, Michael. "The GQ Cover Story: Liam Neeson." *GQ*. April 2014. Web. 30 May 2015.

PART I: A FAMILY AFFAIR

Forms and Functions of Kinship

"Family faces are magic mirrors… we see the past, present, and future."

– Gail Lumet Buckley

Kinship is a culturally constructed system that gauges degree of relatedness between individuals. Cultural standards embedded within systems of kinship serve two purposes: **identifying who belongs** and **how they should behave**. In this section, these functions of kinship will be explored in two parts. Part A provides as overview of the two main types of kinship systems and how relatives are categorized. Part B focuses on how relationships are defined within these groups. The variability of kinship provides a basis for the array of marital systems to be discussed later in the chapter.

A. WE ARE FAMILY?

Identifying Family Members

Kinship systems provide cultural filters that limit group membership, regulate resources (e.g. land), and guide everyday interactions. These systems provide a means of determining who is recognized as family, or part of your lineage. Additionally, they provide categories in which to place and prioritize those viewed as relatives. Limiting and prioritizing group membership is necessary. Biologically, your number of ancestors doubles with every preceding generation. You have two parents, your parents have four parents, and so on. Counting back 20 generations gives you over a million biological relatives! This makes the ability to organize and prioritize relationships necessary for functional society.

There are two main types of kinship systems, generally divided between preindustrial and industrial/ postindustrial societies:

1. **Preindustrial: Patrilineal/Matrilineal**

   Lineage, or family history, is traced through the father's (patrilineal) or mother's (matrilineal) side of the family. This is usually based on which gender controls resources.

   E.g. Maasai of Kenya are pastoralist society in which men own all of the livestock and control access to resources. Children belong to and trace their lineage through their fathers' clans.

2. **Industrial/Postindustrial: Forgetting or ignoring more remote kin groups**

   Importance is based on the relative's proximity to self.

   E.g. The United States is a postindustrial society in which "distant" relatives, usually anyone beyond second cousins, are forgotten. This dictates attitudes about relationships with those beyond these degrees of relatedness.

Members of our kin group are further categorized as either **consanguines** or **affines**. **Consanguineous relatives** are those whom we view as being related by blood. It is important to note that although the term "blood" seems to denote a biological basis, cultural interpretations of biology are not universal. For example, the Canela tribe of Brazil has a category of paternity[3] that is nonexistent in the United States. **One-male**

---

[3] Paternity – Recognized as being the biological father

paternity, or the recognition of one biological father, is common to both groups. However, Canela kinship systems also include belief in partible paternity. **Partible paternity** is the recognition of more than one male as the biological father. Traditional Canela festivals to promote unity within the group included a great deal of sequential and group sex. If pregnancy occurred, all of the partners would be recognized as the child's biological fathers. Both one-male and partible paternity systems influence relationships, such as appropriate daily interactions and potential spouses.

Affines are members of our kin group related through marriage. This was the category in which many placed Allen in regard to Soon-Yi. Contrary to popular opinion, Allen was not Soon-Yi's adoptive father. Soon-Yi was adopted when she was eight years old by Farrow and then-husband, André Previn, in 1978. In 1979, they divorced and Farrow began dating Allen. Since Soon-Yi was a child at this time, some felt this situated Allen as her father figure. However, Allen never legally adopted Soon-Yi and insists that they barely interacted during her childhood. Soon-Yi maintains that she viewed Previn as her father figure. Additionally, since Allen never married Farrow, he was not Soon-Yi's stepfather. Supporters asserted that their relationship was not incestuous by any definition since Allen was neither a consanguineous nor affinal relative. Lack of legal relatedness did not lead to satisfying answers for critics trapped in the discomfort of cultural ambiguity.

B. FAMILY TIES

Degree of Relatedness and Daily Living

Once relatives have been identified, membership is maintained through adherence to appropriate cultural guidelines. This can be complicated, as behaviors must be calibrated with respect to the relationship perceived. These perceptions rely on **degree of relatedness**, a cultural definition of how closely individuals are related. Degree of relatedness is fundamental to determine appropriate interactions between individuals. Perceptions of these connections govern elements of daily living, such as etiquette. These views also impact long-term issues, such as marriage plans and property rights. However, cultural variation can lead to conflicting opinions of what is and is not acceptable.

Rules of appropriateness, such as basic etiquette and taboos, serve as indicators of cultural priorities. Vietnamese culture places a great deal of importance on the use of highly specific titles, especially when addressing relatives. These titles reference gender and age in relation to the speaker. If you were living in southern Vietnam as the youngest of three siblings, the eldest being Sue, it would be viewed as highly disrespectful to call her by first name. The appropriate way to address her would be "Chi Hai," which literally translates into "Older Sister Two." Explanations vary for why the eldest is referred to as two, rather than one. However, all agree on the cultural importance of proper titles in showing respect. This significance of elder status reflected in the title is pervasive to all other interactions, such as restrictions against contradicting older siblings. Many Vietnamese would view the type of bickering viewed as common among siblings in the United States as a major social embarrassment.

Of equal, or some might argue greater, importance are culturally prohibited behaviors, or **taboos**. Taboos regarding incest exist in every kinship system. **Incest**, or sexual interactions between closely related individuals, is often believed to be universal. However, those falling into the category of "closely related" vary between groups. When anthropologist William Crocker brought his wife and two children to visit the Canela tribe in Brazil, they were invited to sit on mats that had been laid out for them. Crocker's 11-year-old daughter and 9-year-old son shared a mat due to limited availability. In the United States, their sharing would have been interpreted as endearing, polite, and even worthy of praise. So the children were confused when the

Canela responded with surprise and laughter. Among the Canela, two opposite-sex siblings sharing a mat was viewed as incestuous.[4]

Cultural variation also exists within the boundaries of the United States, where laws pertaining to marriages between first cousins vary between states. First-cousin marriage is currently legal in 19 states (including New York), as well as Washington, DC. Meanwhile the practice is prohibited in 25 and allowed only under special circumstances in 6.[5]

However, since culture guides behavior more than written law, conflict can arise if interactions are viewed as legal but socially deviant. In the case of Allen and Soon-Yi, disagreement over their degree of relatedness made their relationship's boundaries of appropriateness unclear. For many, ongoing indecision remains over whether Allen was a predator, a playboy, or simply a man in love.

PART II: LOVE AND MARRIAGE

Forms and Functions of Marital Systems

"I love being married. It's so great to find one

special person you want to annoy for the rest of your life."

– Rita Rudner

Marriage is a culturally defined relationship between at least two people. Like kinship, marriage is a system based on and indicative of societal norms and values. It is found in every culture and with astounding variation throughout the world. Evaluation of similarities and contrasts can yield insight into the complexity of human behavior. Assessment reveals that common **primary functions of marriage are**:

1. Forming bonds/alliances between groups for material and social support

    E.g. The Yanomamo tribe of South America often planned marriages as strategically as they planned battle lines.

2. Defining rights and obligations within and around the marriage

    E.g. Prior to marriage, women of the Canela tribe in Brazil traditionally engaged in the Festival Men's Society. This required the woman to engage in sequential sex with 15–20 males, the belief being that it would prepare her to adequately satisfy her husband.

3. Regulation of reproduction and sexual activity

    E.g. New York State requires legal justification for those seeking divorce. Adultery, or consensual sex outside of the marriage, is accepted as valid reason. This reflects mainstream expectations of monogamy within the United States.

---

[4] Crocker, William and Jean G. Crocker. *The Canela: Kinship, Ritual, and Sex in an Amazonian Tribe.* California: Wadsworth, 2004. P. 6.

[5] "State Laws Regarding Marriages Between First Cousins." *National Conference of State Legislatures.* N.p., 2015. Web. 10 July 2015.

Beliefs about kinship directly influence who can marry, who is preferred, and expectations within the marriage (e.g. transfers of wealth). In this section, we will assess four features common to all marriage systems: who can marry; how many; marital exchanges; and cultural expectations. These components of marriage are useful indicators of cultural attitudes and transformations.

A. WHO CAN I MARRY?

The first step in planning a marriage is identifying potential mates. Initial eligibility is based on membership status in various groups. The outcome of this assessment has varied effects based on whether the group is endogamous or exogamous. **Endogamy**, sometimes referred to as in-marriage, means to marry *within* a specific group. Endogamous groups include, but are not limited to, certain tribes, religions, ethnicities, and social classes. An example of strict endogamy exists among the Old Order Amish, a conservative ethno-religious sect with communities dispersed throughout the United States and Canada. Group members are easily identified, as one author stated, "In their olden attire and horse and buggy, the Old Order Amish appear to be driving out of yesterday."[6] The Old Order Amish are forbidden to select mates outside of the group and do not try to recruit new members. Such insularity has provided both advantages and disadvantages. Seclusion instills a powerful sense of group identity and has essentially preserved their culture in its nascent state. However, limited genetic variability has resulted in higher frequency of certain disorders less common among the general population.

Exogamy refers to marriage outside of a specific group. Incest taboos are the most common form of exogamy. Attitudes about kinship directly affect who we view as marriageable. In the United States, those beyond second-cousin status are generally viewed as distant enough to be deemed nonincestuous. For example, in 2013, actor Kevin Bacon and actress Kyra Sedgwick were featured in a PBS program on ancestry. When it was revealed that the pair, married since 1988, were ninth cousins, they responded with general amusement.[7] However, violating cultural requirements of familial exogamy can have disastrous social consequences, including punishment and ejection from the group. These beliefs are often reflected in law, so can also have legal repercussions. Such was the case for German couple Patrick Stübing and Susan Karolewski. Stübing, placed in foster care as a toddler, had no contact with his birth family until reestablishing contact 20 years later in 2000. It was at this time that Stübing, now 23, first met Karolewski, his 16-year-old biological sister. Shortly after, the pair developed an intimate relationship and that was discovered when Karolewski gave birth to their first child in 2001. Referred to in German newspapers as "forbidden lovers of the Fatherland," the pair faced a national ridicule. Stübing was convicted under section 173 of German Criminal Code prohibiting sex between consanguineous siblings and sentenced to three years in prison. The pair has since remained together, have a total of four children, and have remained locked in battles attempting to legalize their union.

Marriage legislation is indicative of cultural attitudes, and in turn, cultural shifts can affect codified laws. The Stübing and Karolewski case has incited widespread debate over the criminalization of incest. Stübing underwent a vasectomy in 2004 in an attempt to strengthen his case and circumvent arguments regarding genetic risks to offspring. In 2014, the German Ethics Council came out in support of Stübing, pointing out that other genetically affected adults were not barred from reproducing. The committee also stated, "Criminal

---

[6] Schaefer, Richard T. and William Zellner. *Extraordinary Groups: An Examination of Unconventional Lifestyles.* 9th Ed. New York: Worth Publishers, 2011. P. 42. Print.

[7] Finding Your Roots. PBS. 3 March 2013. Television.

law is not an appropriate means to preserve a social taboo."[8] Sibling incest is culturally taboo and rare in most of the western world, but incest laws are not consistent in every nation. In France and the Netherlands, consensual incest is not subject to prosecution. The growing debate over incest laws in Germany signifies a shift in cultural attitudes regarding sex and relationships. Differing opinions of the case reflect the immense variety of cultural attitudes that shape marital systems. Another example of cultural shifts affecting legislation is the issue of gay marriage. In recent years, the right for homosexuals to legally marry has become a major source of contention in the United States. At the time of this writing, 37 states legally recognize same-sex couples with activists mounting pressure on those that do not. Changes in marriage legislation mirror the nation's growing cultural shift. **Cultural norms regarding marital eligibility can also serve as a barometer of social change.**

B. HOW MANY CAN I MARRY?

Once eligible potential partners have been identified, cultural standards govern the number of available vacancies. Marital systems reflect cultural values, as exemplified by the strict endogamy of the Old Order Amish discussed in the previous section. This section provides an overview of the most common marriage systems found throughout the world and examples of variation with each: monogamy, polygamy, and group marriage.

1. **Monogamy** – *Two spouses*

   Cultural variation occurs in gender and expectations, as exemplified by differing views on marriage between individuals of the same gender in the United States and throughout the world.

2. **Polygamy** – *More than two spouses; further subdivided into two categories:*

   a) **Polygyny** – One male with multiple wives

   A variant of polygyny is a practice referred to as **nikah misyar**, or the traveler's marriage, which is accepted by some Sunni Muslim communities. Extramarital sex is a religiously based taboo among Sunni Muslims. Nikah misyar is a short-term contract marriage that allows married males to engage in extramarital sex without violating this religious belief.

   b) **Polyandry** – *One female with multiple husbands*

   This has not yet been found to be the most common system in any culture but is viewed as acceptable practice in some. One example of polyandry is in Tibet, where multiple brothers who have inherited land will marry the same woman to keep land from becoming fragmented.

3. **Group marriage** – *multiple males and females*

   Although some researchers view the practice as a rare and fleeting phenomenon, long-term group marriages have been documented. One example was the Kerista Commune in San Francisco. At times numbering in the dozens, members practiced group marriage from approximately 1971 to 1991. Participants formed Best Friend Identity Clusters (BFIC), family groups consisting of multiple spouses. Members practiced **polyfidelity,** or loyalty to the multiple spouses within their BFIC. They are credited with coining the term **compersion,** or "the positive emotion that comes from seeing one's partners enjoying themselves together, the antithesis of jealousy."[9]

---

[8] Huggler, Justin. "Incest a 'fundamental right', German committee says." *The Telegraph.* Telegraph Media Group, 24 Sep. 2014. Web. 12 June 2015. [8]

[9] Hamelin, Larry. "And to No More Settle for Less than Purity: Reflections on the Kerista Commune." *Praxis: Politics in Action* 1.1 (2013): 58–73. Print.

C. MARITAL EXCHANGES

"Marriage is really tough because you have to deal with feelings and lawyers."

– Richard Pryor

Once the appropriate mate or mates have been selected, it is common practice for at least one of the kin groups to provide a gesture of good will. Remember that marriage is often about more than the individual spouses; it is a union of kin groups and communities. Marital exchanges, or the transfer of resources between spousal groups, commonly occur at the beginning of the marriage. If you have ever brought a present to a wedding reception, think of how your relationship to the couple affected your gift choice. Marital exchanges operate in similar fashion, but carry the immense cultural weight of representing the group providing the gift and importance of the union. In this section, we will briefly examine bridewealth and dowry.

Bridewealth is the transfer of wealth from the groom's family to the bride's family. Since this tradition relies on the groom having transferrable wealth, it is most commonly observed among pastoral societies in which men can offer livestock in exchange for brides. While some might interpret this as an economic transaction equivalent to selling brides, the amount of wealth offered can serve as a gauge of the man's ability to provide and care for her. From this vantage point, some might argue that the bride has more power in this dynamic than is immediately evident. **Brideservice** is similar to bridewealth, except that the groom provides labor in place of wealth or goods. Some have proposed that these exchanges are given as a means of compensating the bride's family for losing her as a labor source.[10] However, some have pointed out that this explanation may not apply in societies where women do not contribute significantly to economic systems and production.[11] Ethnographic studies reveal that the dynamics of transferring wealth or labor to the bride's family are far more complex than traditional views of the practice as simply purchasing a wife.

Dowry is the transfer of wealth from the bride's family to the groom's family. Like bridewealth, the gift's value is often associated with social status. However, this can be problematic since dowry is packaged as a component of the bride's worth. Brides may find themselves married to a groom whose primary interest is dowry. This may also lead to a preference for sons, since having a daughter means losing wealth to a groom's family. In India, the tradition has spawned a series of crises, including mass abortion of female fetuses and dowry death. Desperate to avoid the heavy price of dowry, many families chose to abort females leading to an alarming drop in the female population. Another highly disturbing issue of growing concern is dowry death, or sometimes bride-burning. If the husband's family views the dowry as inadequate, the woman may be subjected to horrific abuse and torture. In some cases, the bride's safety may be used to demand more payments. However, it often leads to the woman's death by suicide or, more commonly, homicide. One of the most common methods used to kill women is immolation or bride-burning, a practice to which over 8,000 deaths are attributed to per year. What may surprise some readers is that the Indian government made dowry illegal in 1961 and banned sex determination tests in 1994. However, dowry's cultural weight has led to minimal enforcement and the tradition continues to flourish in every social class.

[10] Schlegel, Alice and Rohn Eloul. "Marriage Transactions: Labor, Property, Status." *American Anthropologist* 90.2 (1988): 291–309.

[11] Jones, Caroline. "Women's Worth: A Western Misconception." *Nebraska Anthropologist* 26 (2011): 96–111.

D. CULTURAL EXPECTATIONS

Marriage functions as a type of social glue between groups providing access to physical and social resources. This makes stability of these bonds a matter of group interest and a useful social barometer. Problems and instability within a group's marital system may be interpreted as indicative of deeper troubles, an example being the oft-discussed growth of divorce in the United States. Additionally, changes in attitudes toward marriage reflect larger shifts in the cultural landscape. This is evident in the debates regarding marriage laws, which some view as obsolete cultural relics. However, a few common denominators exist amid the countless permutations of marriage. In this section, three shared dimensions of marital expectations will be discussed: resource sharing, physical/sexual, and emotional.

1. **Resource Sharing**

    Marriage provides access to physical and social resources, as well as cultural criteria for sharing them. Physical resources are tangible items and wealth, such as livestock and money. Of equal and sometimes greater importance are social resources, which include political alliances and labor. Once access is secured, **marriage systems provide cultural criteria for division of resources**. One example of this is the division of labor between spouses. The division of labor is often indicative of broader cultural attitudes, particularly regarding gender. Therefore, cultural shifts can alter the division of labor in the home. For example, among the Maasai people of Kenya, wives are expected to tend to the livestock and build homes. This is counter to the United States, where construction remains a male-dominated profession and sitcom husbands struggling with home repair is a regular plotline. In recent years, Maasai women have been fighting for access to educational and economic opportunities. This struggle indicates changes in self-identity, or how the Maasai women view themselves.

    Resources are of special consideration to communities in which marriages are arranged. **Arranged marriages** involve mate selection with the guidance of outside parties, usually the parents. Arranged is not synonymous with forced, as most cultures allow potential spouses to reject proposed mates. However, the decision incorporates factors regarding the marriage's impact on the entire group. For example, the 1770 marriage between Louis the XVI of France and Marie Antoinette, born an Austrian Archduchess, was arranged to strengthen ties between their respective nations.

    In modern-day India, the majority of marriages are arranged and family reputation is of utmost importance. Potential mates are intensely scrutinized for compatibility, including details of class, caste, and family history. Surprised to learn that a friend had declined one family's attractive, well-educated daughter as a match for her son, an anthropologist inquired about reasons for rejecting a seemingly perfect candidate. The friend explained that the girl was "too independent" to be happy living in a joint home, a quality that could make life unpleasant for everyone. Such calculated arrangements can seem oppressive and baffling to those who view marriage as founded on romantic love. However, as one young woman explained to a frustrated anthropologist, "My marriage is too important to be arranged by such an inexperienced person as myself… in America the girls are spending all their time worrying… we have the chance to enjoy our life and let our parents do the work and worrying for us." When asked how she could marry a stranger, the woman replied, "If he is a good man, why should I not like him? [If] you know the boy so well before you marry… there will be no mystery and romance. Here, we have the whole of our married life to get to know and love our husband." To the anthropologist, this view of American marriage was a revelation. Contrary to views of arranged marriages as cold calculations, the involvement of potential spouses' families provided emotional dimensions and investment overlooked by the anthropologist.[12] Sharing resources is a seminal component of marriages, and subsequently functions as social glue for communities.

2. Physical/Sexual Expectations

Physical and sexual expectations connected to marriage are often interpreted as biologically rooted or "natural." As a result, individuals who do not adhere to sexual expectations of a culture may cast as abnormal or even criminal. For example, King Louis XIV and Marie Antoinette became a source of intense speculation when 7 years passed before the marriage was consummated. The absence of sex was a deviation from expectations of the arranged union. Socially, whispers of the king's lack of interest with Antoinette fueled rumors regarding his masculinity and mental health. Politically, the marriage had been intended to strengthen the French–Austrian alliance, with an heir serving as the lynchpin.

3. Emotional expectations

Cultural norms established by marital systems have a profound influence on our emotional reactions. Moral and ethical interpretations of marital circumstances occur through culturally constructed filters. However, these views become so inherent to interactions that they are easily misinterpreted as "normal" or universal. Although humans may possess a similar range of emotions, how they are invoked and expressed is subject to great variation. One example of this is the feeling of sexual jealousy. The emotion itself is standard, but the circumstances in which it arises vary immensely between cultures. In societies that traditionally engage in spousal sharing, sexual jealousy would be nonsensical and socially detrimental in many circumstances. Such was the case of Pedro and his wife in *Mending Ways*, a 1999 documentary about the Canela tribe. Although the Canela practice monogamous marriage, extramarital sex with multiple partners is an important feature of some festivals. The atmosphere is celebratory, with men and women enthusiastically participating. But when Pedro's wife prepares to join the festivities, he jealously beats her. Pedro's actions are viewed as an affront to the community and a source of embarrassment to the family. Eventually, his possessiveness results in being ostracized from the tribe.

In recent years, digital technology has resulted in a dramatic transformation of the sociocultural landscape. As a result, spouses are sometimes confronted with uncharted cultural terrain. In 2008, Amy Taylor made headlines when she divorced her husband, David Pollard, after catching him on a couch cuddling with another woman. This was not the first time she had felt betrayed by Pollard, whom she had discovered having sex with a prostitute shortly before they were married. The story may have ended there had it not been for the fact that all of Pollard's infidelities had taken place in an online community known as Second Life.[13] Over 10 million users, including politicians and major corporations, interact in an elaborate three-dimensional digital world through customized avatars. Second Life creates a forum for many users to transcend limitations of the physical realm, such as appearances and behaviors. The Taylor and Pollard divorce may seem like little more than tabloid fodder, but digital interactions wreaking havoc in the physical realm is increasingly common. In 2009, a woman divorced her husband when

---

[12] Nanda, Serena. "Arranging a Marriage in India." *Stumbling Toward Truth: Anthropologists at Work*. Ed. Philip de Vita. Prospect Heights, IL: Waveland, 2000. 196–204. Print.

[13] Morris, Steven. "Second Life Affair Ends in Divorce." *The Guardian*. 13 Nov. 2008. Web. 10 June 2015.

she discovered that his Second Life avatar was "having gay dungeon romps."[14] The burgeoning trend of "cyber-cheating" has inspired some members to establish virtual detective and counseling agencies in the Second Life universe. To some, the lack of physical interaction renders the interactions harmless. Others aligned with the behavior with "emotional cheating."

Despite the current lack of consensus, cultural norms will eventually be recalibrated for navigation of the new terrain. Throughout eons of transformation, systems of kinship and marriage have survived as crucial components of society. The merging of physical and digital worlds will not result in cultural institutions becoming obsolete, only reimagined.

---

[14]Shea, Danny. "Second Life Divorce: Woman Catches Husband in Virtual Gay Affair." *Huff Post Media*. The Huffington Post. 12 Mar. 2009. Web. 10 June 2015.

PRACTICE EXAM QUESTIONS
CHAPTER IV: THE FILMMAKER'S DAUGHTER

T   F   1. <u>Kinship</u> refers to biological lineage or ancestry.

T   F   2. <u>Preindustrial</u> societies commonly use patrilineal or matrilineal systems of kinship.

T   F   3. <u>Endogamy</u> refers to marriage <u>outside</u> of a specific group.

T   F   4. <u>Polyandry</u> refers to one husband with multiple wives.

T   F   5. <u>Bridewealth</u> is a transfer of wealth from the bride's family to the groom's family.

6. Why was Woody Allen and Soon-Yi Previn's relationship controversial?
   a. Previn was already part of an arranged marriage in South Korea
   b. Allen was in a relationship with Previn's adoptive mother
   c. Allen was Previn's adoptive father

7. After Allen and Previn's relationship became public, some decried it as incestuous while others viewed it as a standard Hollywood affair. What basic concept do these differing views illustrate?
   a. Kinship is a cultural construction
   b. Marriage is a cultural construction
   c. Kinship is a biologically based system of ancestry

8. The Maasai people of Kenya are a pastoralist society in which men control all of the resources. Which kinship system do they practice?
   a. Patrilineal
   b. Matrilineal
   c. Unilineal

9. Every culture has a different way of sorting out which relatives are more important. In <u>postindustrial societies,</u> the most common form of doing this is:
   a. Emphasizing/de-emphasizing specific kin groups
   b. Forgetting or ignoring kin beyond first cousins

10. Forgetting or ignoring kin beyond second cousins
   a. The Canela belief in partible paternity allows more than one male to be recognized as a child's biological father. Which type of relatedness does this affect?
   b. Consanguineous
   c. Affines
   d. Patrilineous

11. Woody Allen and Soon-Yi wed in 1997. What type of relatives are they?
   a. Consanguineous
   b. Affines
   c. Patrilineous

12. Degree of relatedness between individuals varies between cultures. As a result, cultural expectations can also shift between cultures. Cultural variation can sometimes lead to embarrassment when norms are unknown. Which example of this occurred during anthropologist William Crocker's visit with the Canela?
    a. He used his male host's hammock, a practice reserved for married couples
    b. His son and daughter sat on the same mat, which the Canela viewed as incestuous
    c. He shared meat with his daughter, a practice reserved for married couples

13. What do America's first-cousin marriage laws say about incest taboos?
    a. They are the same in every state, indicating its biological basis
    b. They vary throughout the states, indicating it is a cultural construction
    c. They vary throughout the states, indicating it has a biological basis

14. The Old Order Amish have a strict practice of marrying <u>within</u> their community. This is referred to as:
    a. Endogamy
    b. Exogamy
    c. Thetan Law

15. The case of Patrick Stübing and Susan Karolewski demonstrates cultural attitudes reflected in legislation. Although the relationship was consensual, why was Stübing jailed under Germany's incest laws?
    a. They are first cousins
    b. They are fraternal twins
    c. They are siblings

16. Nikah misyar, or the "traveler's marriage," is a variation of polygyny. What is this practice?
    a. Long-term marriage in which the groom agrees to a polyandrous arrangement
    b. Short-term marriage allowing Sunni Muslim females to have sex without violating their religious beliefs
    c. Short-term marriage allowing Sunni Muslim males to have sex without violating their religious beliefs

17. During the course of their multidecade group marriage, members of the Kerista Commune popularized terms to describe elements of daily life. One of these terms describes <u>being loyal to multiple partners</u>. This term is:
    a. Compersion
    b. Concession
    c. Polyfidelity

18. In Tibet, brothers will sometimes marry the same woman as means of keeping inherited land together. This form of marriage is referred to as:
    a. Polygyny
    b. Polyandry
    c. Polymonogamy

19. India's government banned dowry in 1961 due to high rates of extortion in which grooms demanded additional payments from the brides' families. However, this culturally significant practice has continued, leading to an estimated 8,000 deaths each year. What is the cause of these dowry-related deaths?
    a. Bride-burning
    b. Suicide
    c. Bride kidnapping

20. When cultural change occurs, it can lead to marital problems regarding differing emotional expectations. Which case was discussed in the text as an example of this?
    a. Divorces over perceived affairs occurring in the online game, *Second Life*
    b. Younger generations of the Old Order Amish secretly dating outsiders
    c. Indian women influenced by western culture and refusing arranged marriages

CHAPTER IV: THE FILMMAKER'S DAUGHTER

1.	False	11.	B
2.	True	12.	B
3.	False	13.	B
4.	False	14.	A
5.	False	15.	C
6.	B	16.	C
7.	A	17.	C
8.	A	18.	B
9.	C	19.	A
10.	A	20.	A

CHAPTER V

SHAKESPEARE'S MAKEOVER: HAWT OR NAWT?

Culture and Language

"2 b, r nt 2 b dat iz d Q

wthr ts noblr n d mnd

2 sufr d slngs & arowz of outrAjs fortn

r 2 tAk armz agnst a C f trblz,

& by oposn nd em?"

Did you recognize the excerpt above? These are the opening lines of the famous soliloquy from Shakespeare's *Hamlet* written in **textspeak**, electronic shorthand consisting largely of abbreviations (e.g. SMH = Shaking My Head). Below is the exact same speech in Early Modern English, its original form:

To be, or not to be? That is the question—

Whether 'tis nobler in the mind to suffer

The slings and arrows of outrageous fortune,

Or to take arms against a sea of troubles,

And, by opposing, end them?

Despite being radically different in appearance, the excerpts are identically worded and indistinguishable if read aloud. But are there more differences than that meets the eye? Is something lost or gained when reading the same words in textspeak? These questions are at the core of an ongoing debate. As textspeak has become ubiquitous to students' lives, educators are faced with its increasing appearance in academic work. Abhorred by some as an irritating obstacle, it has been viewed by others as an opportunity and potential teaching tool. When I ask for students' opinions of this proposal, their diverse responses mirror the vast range of public opinions. Some students are so disturbed that they stop texting just to express visceral disgust with what they see as a lowering of standards. Others practically glow with excitement, viewing it as an adaptive, practical way to connect with the "text generation." As everyone from priests to politicians join the fray, the path to general consensus grows increasingly convoluted.

In 2003, concerns over declining literacy skills were exacerbated after a British teen's essay, written entirely in textspeak, grabbed headlines. The essay's first line, "My smmr hols wr CWOT. B4, we used 2go2 NY 2C my bro, his GF & thr 3 :- kids FTF. ILNY, it's a gr8 plc," was provided by news outlets along with a Standard English translation, "My summer holidays were a complete waste of time. Before, we used to go to New York to see my brother, his girlfriend and their three screaming kids face to face. I love

New York. It's a great place."[1] Among a sea of headlines such as, "TXT BAD 4 UR BRAIN?," this case did little to quell public concern.[2] Educational institutions continue to search for the best way to approach the issue amidst conflicting research and public opinions. Several years later, the Scottish Qualifications Authority was criticized after granting credit for exam answers written in textspeak.[3] Opposition to allow textspeak in academia stems from the potential consequences of normalizing slang. Beyond the potential impact of textspeak on basic literacy skills, many believe that it represents a dangerous "dumbing down" of critical thought and comprehension. Researchers from multiple fields have joined the fray, but studies have yielded mixed results. Some indicate a link between electronic shorthand and a decline in standard literacy skills, including comprehension.[4][5] Others suggest that it is harmless and that slang terms (e.g. OK) have always entered acceptable use in standard language. Some even propose that it is beneficial, stating that switching between the rules of textspeak and standard language yield the same advantages as being bilingual.[6][7]

The textspeak debate is about far more than spelling and grammar. **Language** is a system of nonverbal and verbal symbols that convey meaning within a culture. **Nonverbal communication** consists of body language and physical cues. **Verbal communication** is composed of written and spoken language, including features like accents and grammar. Verbal and nonverbal signals serve as symbols in which we package and transmit cultural traditions (e.g. beliefs). Meanings encoded in language represent cultural concepts to be passed on to subsequent generations. In this sense, language is a cultural tradition and fundamental part of group identity. Subsequently, the textspeak debate is really a deliberation of cultural identity for current and future generations.

Systems of language and culture are bound by a reciprocal relationship. On one side of the equation, language is produced and shaped by culture. While on the other side, cultural views and interactions are influenced by language. At the heart of this relationship is the principle of **linguistic relativity**, commonly referred to as the **Sapir-Whorf Hypothesis**, which posits that language molds our thoughts and how we see the world. The relationship between language and culture is central to how a group regulates language, including educational curricula and censorship. Many fear that what they perceive as substandard language will result in deficient forms of thought. This concern was illustrated in George Orwell's science fiction novel, *1984*, in which a totalitarian government instituted the language of Newspeak. In Orwell's dystopian future, the language of Newspeak omitted words representing contradictory thought. For example, the word "bad" was replaced with "ungood." The implication was that removing the word equated to eliminating the concept. Simplistic language lacking contradictory words was intended to reduce oppositional thoughts, leading to

---

[1] Cramb, Auslan. "Girl writes English essay in phone text shorthand." *The Telegraph*. Telegraph Media Group. 3 Mar. 2003. Web. 1 Jul. 2015.

[2] Waugh, Rob. "TXT BAD 4 UR BRAIN? Text Messaging Can Dent Your Reading Abilities, Say Scientists." *Mail Online*. Associated Newspapers, 17 Feb. 2012. Web. 14 July 2015.

[3] *Daily Mail*. Associated Newspapers Ltd., 1 Nov. 2006. Web. 1 July 2015.

[4] Cingel, Drew P., and S. Shyam Sundar. "Texting, techspeak, and tweens: The relationship between text messaging and English grammar skills." *New Media & Society* 14.8 (2012): 1304–1320.

[5] Lee, Joan Hwechong. *What does txting do 2 language? The influences of exposure to messaging and print media on acceptability constraints*. Diss. University of Calgary, 2011.

[6] Drouin, Michelle, and Claire Davis. "R u txting? Is the use of text speak hurting your literacy?." *Journal of Literacy Research* 41.1 (2009): 46–67.

[7] Powell, Daisy, and Maureen Dixon. "Does SMS text messaging help or harm adults' knowledge of standard spelling?." *Journal of Computer Assisted Learning* 27.1 (2011): 58–66.

a more agreeable, controllable public.[8] Although the degree to which language affects worldview has been a matter of debate, very few would argue that they are completely unrelated. Understanding the link between language and culture allows us to explore the exciting possibilities of language as a potential tool to reconstruct reality and improve our experiences.

This chapter discusses language in four parts. Part I provides an overview of the primary functions of language. Nonverbal language, categorized as body language and physical cues, is discussed in Part II. Part III examines various aspects and influences of verbal language. Part IV is dedicated to the power of nonverbal and verbal language on the unconscious mind.

PART I: FUNCTIONS OF LANGUAGE

1. **Language = Identity.**

    Humans are social primates and "hard-wired" to form groups, but the criteria by which we determine membership are culturally constructed. Cultural beliefs are embedded in the nonverbal and verbal symbols of language. Fluency in language implies cultural familiarity, which indicates *insider* status and position *within* the group, both of which determine access to resources. For example, being able to speak English in the United States identifies you as an insider and can grant you greater access to resources. Your pronunciation may further identify you as being from a specific geographic region, as in the case of distinct Boston accent. In addition to this, the vocabulary and grammatical structure of your speech may be interpreted as a sign of your socioeconomic status and educational background. Language is essential to self-identity, or how we see ourselves, as it creates a bridge connecting us to the belief systems of specific groups. Social identity, how we see others or how others see us, is also informed by our interpretations of language. Our interpretations rely on culturally constructed beliefs about these groups, which can have positive or negative effects on interactions.

2. **Language is a reflection of culture.**

    Language is a barometer of cultural conditions, indicating norms, values, and expectations. Cultural parameters dictate appropriate use and interpretation of language. An example of values reflected in language is the obligatory use of age-based titles in the Vietnamese language. From birth, Vietnamese children learn to utilize appropriate titles when addressing others. These titles indicate the listener's age in relation to the speaker, such as Chi when speaking to an older female. As a result, the child learns to reflexively assess age when evaluating social situations. The incorporation of these titles in language reflects and reinforces the significant role of age in Vietnamese society.

    In addition to dictating appropriate language (e.g. firm handshake), culture also governs the status or value of different forms of language. Consider the disquiet over Shakespeare's texts being filtered into textspeak. Contempt is not directed at deviation from the original, as Shakespeare's works have been subject to many celebrated adaptations. Some readers may be familiar with "Romeo + Juliet," a modern film version in which the families are reimagined as rival criminal organizations and the lovers' famous kiss occurs in an elevator.[9] Compared to deviations in plot and wording, the presentation of *Hamlet* in textspeak is quantitatively minute. Much of the disdain is directed at the use of textspeak, viewed by

---

[8] Orwell, George. *1984*. Ed. Erich Fromm. New York: Harcourt, 1949.

[9] *Romeo + Juliet*. Dir. Baz Luhrmann. Perf. Leonardo DiCaprio and Claire Danes. 20th Century Fox, 1996.

some as a little more than low-culture[10] slang. Although Shakespeare's work is interspersed with slang and idioms of his era, these expressions are interpreted as formal in the modern context.

Current cultural values create standards of formal language leading us to perceive various forms, such as textspeak, as positive or negative. Consider how you might view the Early Modern English version of Shakespeare if the original text had been written in textspeak. To some, the use of textspeak in academia is an indicator and agent of intellectual decline that must be eliminated. Others view it as part of the ongoing evolution of language that should be embraced as an opportunity to develop new teaching methods.

3. **Language is an indicator of cultural change.**

Cultural needs shape methods of communication, which have an impact on how we perceive and use language. Subsequently, fluctuations in language coincide with shifts in the cultural landscape. Changes in communication may be prompted by a plethora of factors, such as migration or technology. New forms of language linked to specific groups, such as ethnic or generational (e.g. Textspeak among Millennials), give rise to changes in self and social identity. Assessing part and current variations can yield insights into history, cultural development, and identity formation.

Physical movement, such as migration or trade routes, leads to interactions that give rise to cultural exchanges and creations. Resulting modifications are embedded in language, leaving cultural footprints that can be analyzed in a number of ways. Extended contact between groups, such as through trade, generates means of intergroup communication. Simplified language structures used to facilitate understanding with other groups are referred to as **pidgin**. An example of pidgin is Chinook Jargon, a modified version of native language formerly used by Native Americans in the Northwest to communicate with traders. Extended contact can lead to pidgin entering common use by an established group, a stage in which the language is referred to as a **creole**.[11] A well-known example of this is Louisiana Creole French (LCF), a system stemming from contact between multiple cultural groups during the era of slavery. Structural assessments (e.g. grammar) of LCF reveal its origins during early stages of the slave trade. Barriers presented by distinct languages spoken by slaves from various African groups were overcome as the emergence of Afro-Creole identity yielded a shared language. This language reflected shared cultural beliefs and values among the disadvantaged class, allowing them to organize and conspire against the ruling French class.[12] LCF's roots among the dispreferred class remains evident in ongoing negative cultural stereotypes of its speakers.[13] These perceptions can lead to assumptions about educational background and general competence.[14] Evaluation of LCF's development provides information pertaining to historical origins and cultural identity of its speakers.

The emergence of textspeak is a reflection of changing cultural needs. Postindustrialism is a socioeconomic adaptation in which focus is placed on service, creating a need for instant communication. Subsequently, e-communication became ubiquitous to daily life, dissolving the boundary between digital and physical realms. Accordingly, expressions and informal style of textspeak migrated into common

---

[10]**Low-culture:** Artifacts and traditions associated with lower socioeconomic class; Often associated with vulgarity and lack of education.

[11]Blackshire-Belay, C. "The location of Ebonics within the framework of the africological paradigm." *Journal Of Black Studies*, 27.1 (1996): 5–23.

[12]Valdman, Albert. *French and Creole in Louisiana*. Springer Science & Business Media, 1997. p. 337.

[13]Carlisle, Aimee Jeanne. *Language Attrition in Louisiana Creole French*. Diss. University of California, Davis, 2010.

[14]Brown, Becky. "The social consequences of writing Louisiana French." *Language in Society* 22.01 (1993): 67–101.

language. Textspeak has become so common to daily interactions that some expressions have been recognized in *The Oxford English Dictionary*.[15] Along with the introduction of textspeak into standard lexicon, the abbreviated fashion of e-communication has also decreased the formality of many interactions. I am often able to guess the age range of students based on the format of their e-mails. To those who grew up prior to the era of texting, e-mail was viewed as an equivalent to standard letters. Because of this, students of this generation tend to format messages like formal letters, opening with "Dear Professor" and ending with a "Sincerely." For students born into a world where smartphones are standard, e-mail falls into the same category as texting. Students of this generation tend to format e-mails much like casual text messages, usually containing only the body or single question. To some, this may be interpreted as inappropriate or even disrespectful. While to others, the absence of formality saves time by getting directly to the point and may be viewed as a courtesy to everyone involved. The value that is placed on formalities, such as opening with "Dear Professor," is gauged by the reader's cultural interpretations. Some instructors are incensed by the lack of formality, viewing it as unprofessional and a sign of social decay, while other, often younger, educators are unfazed and see e-mail as an appropriate forum for casual communication.

The view of abbreviated communications as an insult or a courtesy relies on the cultural background of the recipient. This range of perceptions is a product of the rapid change introduced by digital interactions, thrusting us into social territory in which cultural guidelines are still being established. The continuing debates regarding the use of textspeak in academia is rooted in the current lack of cultural consensus. Disagreement over the value of various components of language complicates the creation of educational procedures for large groups.

PART II: NONVERBAL LANGUAGE

Nonverbal communication accounts for the majority of the messages conveyed in daily interactions. Most of our opinions about others and their perceptions of us are already formulated before any words have been exchanged. This is not to say that your words do not matter, but that your nonverbal signals can significantly help or hinder the message you are trying to send. In this section, we will discuss the two components of nonverbal communication: body language and physical cues.

a. Body Language

Body language is a short-term indicator of immediate emotional states. Studies of body language are categorized as kinesics, oculesics, and proxemics. **Kinesics**, a term coined by American Anthropologist Ray Birdwhistell, is the systematic study of body movements and gestures.[16] **Oculesics** is the study of use and interpretation of eye contact in various settings. Interpretations of body language are governed by cultural norms and expectations. **Proxemics** describes perceptions and utilization of interpersonal space. A wealth of information is conveyed voluntarily and involuntarily through our nonverbal signals. Voluntary body language is used to express intended messages. Involuntary body language, which occurs without our awareness or control, can reveal underlying emotions that may or may not coincide

---

[15] Lee, Amy. "LOL, OMG, ♥ Added To The Oxford English Dictionary." *The Huffington Post*. TheHuffingtonPost.com. 24 Mar. 2011. Web. 1 June 2015.

[16] Birdwhistell, Ray L. *Introduction to Kinesics*. Louisville, KY: U of Louisville, 1952. 2.

with the message intended. In this section, the impacts of voluntary and involuntary body language will be explored.

Voluntary body language involves the movements and gestures intentionally used to send specific messages. Culture provides guidelines for the nonverbal cues used to represent emotions and ideas. Adherence to these parameters can reveal your cultural background, identifying you as an insider or outsider. For example, consider the wealth of information embedded in the brief act of handshaking. While viewed as a standard social practice in some cultures, it is nonexistent or even distasteful in others. Handshaking cultures also display immense variation in rules surrounding the tradition, such as when and with whom it is appropriate. In American culture, this fleeting, nonverbal cue contains a multitude of parameters and pitfalls. Factors such as the firmness of your grip and eye contact are assessed according to cultural standards. If you did not grow up in a handshaking culture, you may be totally unaware of the multiple signals encoded in this momentary act. In the United States, a limp handshake is viewed as a sign of passivity or lack of confidence. In China and South Korea, where a softer handshake is preferred, a firm handshake can be interpreted as overly aggressive or disrespectful.

The messages purposely conveyed through voluntary body language are interpreted by the conscious mind and influenced by beliefs in the unconscious. At the conscious level, you may be pleased that a job applicant provided a firm handshake. However, cultural beliefs embedded in the unconscious mind also influence our perceptions. One example of this is the influence of cultural belief about gender on interpretations of the same behaviors. In a study published in 2000, "Handshaking, gender, personality, and first impressions," the handshakes of 112 subjects were assessed for personality and impact on the experimenters' perceptions. Firmer handshakes were positively related to extraversion and emotional openness, while weaker handshakes were linked to shyness and neuroticism. Men generally had a firmer handshake than women, but the correlation between style and personality traits was consistent for both genders. Accordingly, women displaying a firmer handshake tended to make a more positive impression on experimenters.[17] This finding was unique to other studies in which women exhibiting confidence using the same behaviors, such as speaking style, as men were perceived negatively.[18] According to the researchers, handshaking can serve as an effective means of conveying confidence without the negative repercussions incurred by other methods.

Involuntary body language occurs and is interpreted without our conscious awareness. A common example is referred to by poker players as a "tell." Tells are gestures or facial expressions that reveal concealed emotions. These are visible indicators that can be used to gauge a person's honesty, a valuable tool when playing a game like poker. For example, you might notice that every time Johnny narrows his eyes and purses his lips whenever he is dealt a poor hand. However, he may attempt to trick others into thinking that he has good cards by constantly raising his bet. Thinking he has a strong hand, everyone folds and leaves you as Johnny's last opponent. Johnny continues to bluff and goes all in, putting all of his money into the pot. This risky move is intended to convey confidence in his hand, but knowing that Johnny has a weak hand reveals it as a bluff. You stay the course, win the game, and take all of Johnny's money. Tells are commonly associated with card players, but we send messages through involuntary body language all the time. The examples we will discuss are microexpressions and pupillary dilation.

---

[17]Chaplin, William F., et al. "Handshaking, gender, personality, and first impressions." *Journal of personality and social psychology* 79.1 (2000): 110.

[18]Carli, Linda L. "Gender, language, and influence." *Journal of Personality and Social Psychology* 59.5 (1990): 941.

Microexpressions are momentary facial, subtle expressions that reveal concealed emotions. In the 1970s, behaviorists developed the **Facial Action Coding System (FACS)**, a method of detecting and analyzing microexpressions. Muscle groups are assigned to numbered categories or "action units" (AU) based on facial expression produced and designated by numbers. For example, the muscles that raise the inner eyebrow are referred to as AU1, while those that raise the outer brow are AU2.[19] Activation of an AU, alone or combined with others, indicates underlying emotions. The FACS serves a manual for detecting and interpreting microexpressions that occur within fractions of a second.[20] Television shows have popularized this concept by portraying fictional detectives as "human lie detectors." While this makes for compelling entertainment, microexpressions must be analyzed with consideration to cultural and social context. For example, imagine that a woman's microexpression indicates concealed fear while being questioned by a male detective. This not an automatic sign that she is afraid of being caught in a lie. If she comes from a culture in which being alone with an unrelated man is taboo, her discomfort may stem from the inappropriate nature of the situation. Although reading microexpressions is complicated, it remains a useful tool in behavior-based fields, such as psychology and criminal justice.

Another example of involuntary body language is **pupillary dilation**, or expansion of the black dot in the center of your iris. Dilation of the pupils occurs in response to heightened emotional states, such as fear or sexual arousal. Although this is a biological trait, occurrence relies on cultural interpretations and subsequent emotional reactions. We unconsciously detect and respond to pupillary dilation, particularly in regard to potential mates. In an experiment conducted by Dr. Eckhard Hess, 20 heterosexual male subjects were presented two seemingly identical images of a woman's face. The subjects were not aware that the only difference between the pictures was that one had been retouched to enlarge her pupils. The men exhibited greater pupillary dilation in response to the retouched image, indicating more interest or attraction. Some reported more positive impressions from the altered photo and perceived the woman's facial expression as being different. These subjects were surprised to learn that the only difference had been pupil size.[21] Detection of and response to pupil size may be an evolutionary trait linked to sexual selection. For males, pupillary dilation in females indicates interest and greater potential as a mate. In 2004, a study revealed slightly more complicated effects of pupil size on the sexual preferences of females. Females reported a consistent preference for males with medium to large pupils. However, females drawn to males with larger pupils reported a history of dating "bad boy" types.[22] Variation in female preferences may result from an association between heightened interest indicated by dilated pupils and aggression. A 2009 study found a correlation between fertility and mate preference. Women in the fertile phase of their menstrual cycle showed significantly stronger preference for males with larger pupil size.[23]

The involuntary nature of pupillary dilation has been put to use in various cultures. During the Middle Ages, Italian women used belladonna to dilate their pupils and increase attractiveness. Despite its many toxic effects, this risky practice was popular and "belladonna" means beautiful woman in

---

[19] Ekman, Paul, and Erika L. Rosenberg. *What the face reveals: Basic and applied studies of spontaneous expression using the Facial Action Coding System (FACS)*. Oxford University Press, 1997. P. 12.

[20] Ekman, Paul, and Wallace V. Friesen. "Facial action coding system." (1977).

[21] Hess, Eckhard H. "Attitude and pupil size." *Scientific American* (1965).

[22] Tombs, Selina, and Irwin Silverman. "Pupillometry: A sexual selection approach." *Evolution and Human Behavior* 25.4 (2004): 221–228.

[23] Caryl, Peter G., et al. "Women's preference for male pupil-size: Effects of conception risk, sociosexuality and relationship status." *Personality and Individual Differences* 46.4 (2009): 503–508.

Italian. Atropine, a derivative of belladonna, is currently used to treat a variety of conditions along with inducing pupillary dilation.[24] Another example of the use of this involuntary reflex was documented among seasoned jade dealers in China. Experienced vendors would use the pupils of prospective buyers as an indicator of the products that interested them. In response, some buyers began wearing dark glasses during these negotiations.[25]

Culture shapes perceptions of body language at the conscious and unconscious levels. Cultural standards of social interaction, such as boundaries of interpersonal space, become so habitual that we may be unaware of them. An example of this occurred during a conversation with a friend from Italy. Italian culture is categorized as high-contact, meaning that social interactions involve a great deal of physical touching and less distance is kept between individuals during interactions. By comparison, Americans have a low-contact culture in which more distance is expected between individuals. During our discussion, I automatically positioned myself about three feet away from him. Accustomed to a shorter distance during conversations, he moved slightly closer without realizing it. As a result and without my awareness, I stepped back. This involuntary dance continued without our awareness until we found ourselves halfway across the room! My feeling of being crowded occurred without conscious awareness and caused me to step back without realizing it. Conflicting cultural norms can significantly hinder communication in crucial situations, such as health care. Awareness of these variations is essential in engaging with those from other cultural backgrounds in personal and professional settings.

b. **Physical Cues**

Physical cues are long-term indicators of status, such as age and health. Interpretations of physical cues are shaped by both biology and culture. An example of this combined effect exists in perceptions of female attractiveness. Ideal traits are those that are indicative of sexual receptivity and/or fertility. These preferences are rooted in biology, but refined and differentiated by culture. A universal preference revealed by cross-cultural studies is low waist-to-hip ratio (WHR), or small waist paired with wider hips. Estrogen, a hormone crucial to female fertility, suppresses fat deposits in the abdomen and stimulates distribution in the hips. Thus, a low WHR is indicative of increased estrogen and fertility. A predilection for low WHR may have developed as an evolutionary adaptation allowing males to gauge female fertility.[26]

Shared preferences are rare in comparison to diverse standards of female attractiveness. Preferences in overall body type are influenced by resource availability. In societies prone to food shortages or famine, heavier body types are preferred. This may have developed as an adaptation, since a female with higher fat stores would have greater reproductive success amid resource scarcity.[27] However, in developed nations, a preference for plumper body types is linked to lower socioeconomic status.[28] How we alter physical cues, such as through plastic surgery, serves as an indicator of status and social

[24] Hess, Eckhard H., and Slobodan B. Petrovich. "Pupillary behavior in communication." *Nonverbal behavior and communication* (1987): 327–348.

[25] Gump, Richard. *Jade: stone of heaven.* Doubleday, 1962.

[26] Singh, Devendra. "Adaptive significance of female physical attractiveness: role of waist-to-hip ratio." *Journal of personality and social psychology* 65.2 (1993): 293.

[27] Ford, Clellan S., and Frank A. Beach. "Patterns of sexual behavior." (1951).

[28] Sobal, Jeffery. "Obesity and socioeconomic status: a framework for examining relationships between physical and social variables." *Medical anthropology* 13.3 (1991): 231–247.

structure. Statistics regarding plastic surgery trends in various nations reveal characteristics viewed as culturally ideal. These traits are generally associated with mainstream cultural standards and status.

PART III: VERBAL LANGUAGE

Verbal language refers to written and spoken symbols that are culturally defined. These cultural definitions influence how we make sense of the world, including how we see ourselves and others. Verbal language provides culturally constructed guideposts that we use to categorize and define the world. As a result, the language we speak can literally determine how we see. For example, there is variation in how Russian and English speakers divide the color spectrum. In English, the word "blue" can be broadly applied to a vast spectrum from light to dark. The Russian language does not have a generic, all-encompassing term for blue. When Russian-speaking children learn to identify colors, there is a requisite distinction made between light blue ("goluboy") and dark blue ("siniy"). When native speakers of each language were asked to classify various shades of blue as either light or dark, Russian speakers completed the task significantly faster than English speakers.[29] Although subjects were presented with the same array of colors, the distinction between light and dark blue was part of the immediate interpretation for the Russian speakers. Cultural categories reflected in language become inherent to our perceptions. These patterns are so deeply ingrained in how we think, that they feel instinctual or "natural." As a result, the power of cultural influence in daily living is often underestimated or unnoticed.

In addition to expressing and transmitting cultural concepts, verbal language has profound impacts on formation of self and social identity. The use of language as an evaluative tool to distinguish group members from strangers begins in early infancy. Studies indicate that the ability to identify native dialect arises as early as five months of age.[30] In addition to recognizing dialect, infants look longer at individuals who have previously spoken their language in a native accent, as opposed to non-native accent.[31]

Verbal cues, such as regional accents and dialects, shape perceptions of status based on learned cultural stereotypes. **Accents,** commonly linked to specific geographic regions, signal status primarily through specific styles of pronunciation. Two people speaking the same language may have different accents, despite using the same words. Accents may identify a person as a native or non-native speaker. **Dialects** are variations from standard language that are systematic and unique to specific groups (e.g. regions, class, gender). Dialects are characterized by differences such as vocabulary, accent, and grammatical structure. An example of this would be American English and British English. A *flashlight* in American English is referred to as a *torch* in British English. Categorizing a style of speech as a distinct dialect requires the identification of consistent, systematic patterns. Recognition of these features is subject to interpretation, leading to conflicting views of what constitutes dialect. This is demonstrated by disagreement among Social Scientists over the number of dialects in the United States, with estimates ranging from 3 to over 30.

---

[29] Winawer, Jonathan, et. al. "Russian blues reveal effects of language on color discrimination." *Proceedings of the National Academy of Sciences* 104.19 (2007): 7780–7785.

[30] Nazzi, T., Jusczyk, P., & Johnson, E. "Language discrimination by English-learning 5-month-olds: Effects of rhythm and familiarity." *Journal of Memory and Language* 43 (2000): 1–19.

[31] Kinzler, K.D., et. al. "The native language of social cognition." *Proceedings of the National Academy of Sciences of the United States of America* 104 (2007): 12577–12850.

Of the more commonly recognized dialects is African American Vernacular English (AAVE), sometimes referred to as Ebonics. One of the most distinct features of AAVE is the use of double or multiple negatives for emphasis, a grammatically unacceptable mechanism in SAE.[32] Divergent rules yield highly contrasting versions of similar sentences, as demonstrated in the following comparisons:

Example 1.
AAVE: **She ain't got no coat.**
SAE: **She doesn't have a coat.**

Example 2.
AAVE: **That wasn't not funny.**
SAE: **That wasn't funny.**

As with all forms of language, AAVE signals cultural familiarity and social status. Although there are variations of AAVE, its primary features are fixtures in African American communities. Its commonality crosses geographic and social divides, such as economic status. In this way, it can be emblematic of African American unity and cultural identity. However, AAVE is also associated with negative cultural stereotypes that can diminish opinions of the speaker's intelligence and competence. Adverse perceptions of AAVE speakers present disadvantages in a multitude of crucial environments. For example, studies show that educators commonly have unfavorable views of AAVE and lower expectations of its speakers.[33] Despite efforts to provide an environment conducive to learning for all students, the effects of negative perceptions often occur unintentionally. Low expectations eventually result in a decreased demand for work and effort, resulting in fewer constructive interactions between teachers and students. The detrimental effects of low expectations on student-teacher interactions include:

- Tendency to seat students further away from the instructor or in a group[34][35]
- Briefer, less informative feedback [36]
- Increased frequency of criticism for failure and less praise for success.[37]

In general, low-expectation students receive less attention and encouragement. As a result, these students may fail at higher rates further reinforcing preconceived notions. Resulting bias can lead to a myriad of disadvantages, including lower selection for employment.[38]

---

[32] Martin, Stefan, et al. "The Sentence in African American Vernacular English." *African American English: structure, history, and use* (1998): 11–36.

[33] Smith-Price, Julie. *Why Do They Talk that Way?: Teachers' Perceptions of the Language Young Students Bring Into the Classroom.* Ann Arbor: ProQuest LLC, 2009.

[34] Good, T. L. "Teacher expectations and student perceptions: A decade of research." *Educational Leadership* 38.5 (1981): 415–421.

[35] Rist, R. "Student social class and teacher expectations: The self-fulfilling prophecy in ghetto education." *Harvard Educational Review* 40 (1970): 411–451.

[36] Cooper, H. "Pygmalion grows up: A model for teacher expectation communication and performance influence." *Review of Educational Research* 49.3(1979): 389–410.

[37] Brophy, J. E., and Good, T. L. "Teachers' communication of differential expectations for children's classroom performance." *Journal of Educational Psychology* 61.5 (1970): 365–374.

[38] Cocchiara, Faye K. *Sociolinguistic cues, perceived race and employment selection outcomes: An exploration of the aversive racism framework.* ProQuest, 2007.

Language is the cultural code of a group, but we move between multiple realities every day. This requires the ability to adhere to a variety of communication styles to signal insider status. Shifting between systems of language is referred to as **code-switching**. Code-switching requires the capacity to understand and implement different sets of cultural rules. This necessitates familiarity with the specific culture and its social implications. Discussions of code-switching often focus on bi- or multilingual individuals, such as immigrants. For example, children of immigrants in the United States may speak English while at school, but speak native tongue at home. However, code-switching also happens when we move between social contexts. The comedy sketch show, *Key & Peele*, demonstrated social code-switching in a bit depicting two men on cell phones. While on the phone with his wife, one man's speech is softer and more standardized. When he notices that another man has come within earshot, his voice deepens and he shifts into a slang-based "street" style of speaking culturally associated with toughness. However, this code-switch allows him to indirectly signal his status to the other man.

The practice of code-switching requires deep knowledge of the cultural values entrenched in the language. This can trigger **frame-switching**, a change in the overall cultural lens used to interpret events and experiences. In one study, 80 Chinese–Americans with deep knowledge of both cultures were asked to watch a video avatar providing instructions for a task, which was to interpret an image. Subjects were unaware that some heard the instructions in Chinese-accented English, while others heard them in an American English accent. Subjects were then presented with a picture of a school of fosh in which one fish is positioned in front of the others. Those who had heard the instructions with a Chinese accent tended to view the group of fish as working together to chase the lone fish. Subjects who heard the instructions with an American English accent tended to view the lone fish as leading the other fish. This reflects collectivist values typical of Chinese culture, which contrasts with the more individualistic standpoint of American culture. Simply hearing the accent induced a cultural frame switch, influencing how subjects interpreted the same image.[39]

PART IV: THE UNCONSCIOUS MIND

The cultural meaning we attribute to nonverbal and verbal symbols influences us consciously and unconsciously. The **conscious mind** is home to rational thought processes within our scope of awareness and control. Below this domain, the **unconscious mind** contains instantaneous reactions that affect perceptions in ways of which we are often unaware. Unconscious thought patterns are guided by cultural beliefs, which profoundly influence expectations, interactions, and outcomes. This makes consideration of the cultural meaning attributed to symbols of language critical. Two ways in which culturally constructed meanings influence us at the unconscious level are implicit association and priming.

a. **Implicit Association**

Implicit association refers to the automatic associations we make between symbols and ideas. In the unconscious mind, verbal and nonverbal cues trigger culturally constructed patterns of thought. Imagine riding a bicycle down the same dirt path every day. Habitually, you ride in the same pattern and a rut forms. Now whenever you ride on that path, you are more likely to naturally drift into the pathway formed by the rut. Our minds operate in a similar fashion, but with patterns of thought. Let us say that you grow up in a culture in which African American males are stereotyped as criminals. If

---

[39] Dehghani, Morteza, et al. "The Subtlety of Sound Accent as a Marker for Culture." *Journal of Language and Social Psychology* (2014): 0261927X14551095.

this idea is reinforced through cultural cues, such as mainstream media, this is similar to creating a rut in your mind. Consciously, you may understand that not all African American males are criminals. However, your unconscious mind is quicker to make the association between negative behavior and African American males. Implicit associations are triggered by a multitude of verbal (e.g. accent) and nonverbal cues (e.g. gender).

The influence of implicit associations may seem subtle, but can have major consequences on reactions and outcomes. These can make major differences in crucial situations, such as those requiring split-second decisions. Consider the many situations in which police officers are forced to react instantly. Imagine being a police officer and encountering a man in a darkened alley. The man appears to be pulling something out of his pocket. Although it is hard to see exactly what it is, your mind automatically fills in the blank. Like the rut causing your bicycle to naturally follow a certain path, culturally constructed implicit associations influence what your mind sees in the dark. If your unconscious mind makes an implicit association between black males and danger, it is more likely that you will perceive a gun instead of a wallet. That can make the difference between waiting a few extra seconds or firing automatically; literally, life and death.

Despite the popular belief that we choose our perceptions, everyone makes implicit associations without being aware of it. In 1998, researchers from the University of Washington introduced the **Implicit Association Test (IAT)**. This computer-based test analyzes the amount of time taken to connect specific words and images. The amount of time it takes to correctly categorize items reveals which ideas are more difficult for your mind to connect. As a result, the test reveals your mind's "ruts" or underlying biases that can make you more likely to interpret experiences in certain ways.[40] For example, the test for gender bias is used to see if your mind is quicker to associate males, as opposed to females, with the workplace. In the first round, the category on the left is "Male OR Career" and "Female OR Family." You must correctly categorize words that flash in the center of the screen by matching them with the target words in either category. In the second round, you complete the same task with the categories "Male OR Family" and "Female OR Career." Since traditionally, males have been associated with work and females with the home, most subjects take fractionally longer to correctly categorize words when the ideas are switched. The IAT reveals the strength of underlying bias based on differences in time. This test, available free online, can be used to gain insight into implicit associations pertaining to a wide array of categories, such as disability and religion.

b. **Priming**

Priming is the act of the triggering implicit associations using various cues. Signals can be used intentionally to influence perceptions, thoughts, and behaviors. However, culture shapes the meaning of symbols that stimulate implicit associations. Exposure to specific verbal or nonverbal stimuli can guide our thoughts in significant ways.

An example of how quickly priming can affect perception and behavior was demonstrated by a study on the effects of exposure to words linked to old age and walking speed. Thirty students were asked to unscramble a series words to form a sentence. However, some students received sentences containing words related to old age, such as "Florida" and "wrinkled." Additionally, students were unaware that the speeds at which they entered and exited the room were being timed. Results showed that students exposed to words involving old age walked out of the room at a significantly slower pace than those who

---

[40] Greenwald, Anthony G., Debbie E. McGhee, and Jordan LK Schwartz. "Measuring individual differences in implicit cognition: the implicit association test." *Journal of personality and social psychology* 74.6 (1998): 1464.

had not. The inherent cultural association between words indicating old age and frailty unconsciously influenced the students' movements.[41] While these results may not seem significant, think about how easily the students' behaviors were influenced without their awareness. We are primed by cultural signals all of the time and without our awareness. Now consider the collective power of priming over the course of a year, lifetime, or generation.

In a study published in 2004, subjects were asked to identify weapons in a series of images. Before beginning the test, subjects were unknowingly primed with images of black or white male faces. Results showed that subjects primed with images of black males were not only quicker to identify weapons, but also more likely to incorrectly identify other items as weapons. Related studies also showed that seeing a black male face prior to the test also increased likelihood of subjects interpreting scenes and images as aggressive. This pattern was present among both black and white test subjects, some of whom were police officers.[42] Culturally constructed stereotypes give rise to implicit associations, such as the link between black males and violence. These implicit associations are activated by culturally defined cues that come to symbolize these stereotypes and affect our interactions. The cumulative effects of priming can shape patterns of interaction, leading to conflicts within the larger social structure.

Priming and implicit associations influence social identity, as well as how we see ourselves. This can have major implications for success in academic and occupational fields. A 2008 study revealed that the implicit, cultural associations made between white lab coats and ability could influence performance in simple cognitive tests. When tasked with identifying differences between two images, subjects wearing the lab coat consistently outperformed those who were not. Additionally, they outperformed subjects wearing white painters' coats, which appear similar to lab coats but lack the culturally symbolic meaning.[43]

[41] Bargh, John A., Mark Chen, and Lara Burrows. "Automaticity of social behavior: Direct effects of trait construct and stereotype activation on action." *Journal of personality and social psychology* 71.2 (1996): 230.

[42] Eberhardt, Jennifer L., et al. "Seeing black: race, crime, and visual processing." *Journal of personality and social psychology* 87.6 (2004): 876.

[43] Adam, Hajo, and Adam D. Galinsky. "Enclothed cognition." *Journal of Experimental Social Psychology* 48.4 (2012): 918–925.

PRACTICE EXAM QUESTIONS
CHAPTER V: SHAKESPEARE'S MAKEOVER: HAWT OR NAWT?

T F 1. The <u>Sapir-Whorf Hypothesis</u> states that language influences our thoughts and how we see the world.

T F 2. <u>Pidgin</u> is a simplified language structure used to facilitate communication between groups with different native languages.

T F 3. <u>Physical cues</u> are long-term indicators of status, such as sex or age.

T F 4. The Implicit Association Test reveals biases of the <u>conscious</u> mind.

T F 5. <u>Code-switching</u> is the act of shifting between systems of language.

6. In 2003, a British teen's essay grabbed headlines and fueled debates about the literacy skills of upcoming generation. Why was her essay so controversial?
   a. She wrote it in textspeak, which prompted debates about its use in schools
   b. She wrote each paragraph in a different language, sparking debates about the benefits and drawbacks of learning foreign languages in schools
   c. Her essay contained a large amount of profane words and images. This prompted debates regarding freedom of expression

7. How did Newspeak, in Orwell's <u>1984</u>, demonstrate the Sapir-Whorf Hypothesis?
   a. Complex, adverse language was promoted to stimulate intellectual thoughts
   b. Hostile, fearful language was promoted to boost aggression against outsiders
   c. Simple, agreeable language was promoted to discourage contradictory thought

8. Which aspect of language is illustrated by the ongoing debate over the effects of textspeak and its use in academia?
   a. Cultural beliefs influence legislation and official protocols
   b. Language is an indicator of cultural beliefs and changes
   c. All of the above

9. What do current cultural perceptions of Louisiana Creole French (LCF) speakers reveal about its origins during the slave trade?
   a. Negative stereotypes of LCF speakers reflect origins among the dispreferred class
   b. Positive stereotypes of LCF speakers reflect origins among the elite, ruling class
   c. Negative stereotypes of LCF speakers reflect origins among the elite, ruling class

10. Which component of language includes kinesics, oculesics, and proxemics?
   a. Verbal language
   b. Body language
   c. Physical cues

11. Studies have shown that women who exhibit confidence in the same ways as men, such as speaking style, are perceived negatively. What was discovered in the study "Handshaking, gender, personality, and first impressions"?

    a. Women with firm handshakes were perceived negatively, proving that cultural perceptions of gender are primary to first impressions

    b. Women with firm handshakes were perceived positively, suggesting this as a way for women to convey confidence without being perceived negatively

    c. Women with weak handshakes were perceived positively because it implied a nurturing personality

12. The Facial Action Coding System assigns numbers to various muscle groups of the face. Using this system, trained experts are able to detect and analyze fleeting, involuntary facial expressions. These expressions are believed to reveal true, underlying emotions and are referred to as:

    a. Microexpressions

    b. Miniexpressions

    c. Macroexpressions

13. Dr. Eckhard Hess conducted a study gauging the level of attraction reported by male subjects in response to nearly identical images of a woman. Subjects reported greater interest in the retouched photo in which the woman had:

    a. A slightly broader smile

    b. Constricted pupils

    c. Dilated pupils

14. Studies examining the link between male pupil size and female perceptions of attractiveness yielded some surprising results. Which traits were consistent to females who preferred large pupils?

    a. History of dating "bad boy" types and/or were in fertile phase of menstrual cycle

    b. History of dating "strong, silent" and/or were in fertile phase of menstrual cycle

    c. History of dating "bad boy" types and/or not in fertile phase of menstrual cycle

15. Physical cues consistently deemed as universally attractive imply biological origins. Which cross-culturally preferred trait, discussed in the text, do some researchers suggest evolved as a means for male to gauge female fertility?

    a. Low waist-to-hip ratio

    b. Long legs and narrow feet

    c. Intermembral index (IMI) greater than 120

16. Cultural differences lead to immense variation in which physical cues are viewed as attractive. According to studies discussed in the text, what is the correlation between resource availability and preferred female body type?

    a. Societies with a history of nomadism prefer leaner, muscular body type

    b. Societies prone to food shortages or famine prefer plumper body type

    c. Societies with abundant food sources prefer plumper body type

17. Studies show that educators have unfavorable perceptions of African American Vernacular English (AAVE). How does this affect AAVE-speaking students?
    a. Lower expectations of AAVE speakers lead to less attention and encouragement
    b. Concern for AAVE speakers leads to unwanted attention, or being "singled out"
    c. Higher expectations of AAVE speakers lead to unreasonable demands

18. In a study of frame-switching among Chinese-Americans, how did subjects who heard the instructions with a Chinese accent interpret an image of fish?
    a. Lone fish was leading the other fish (i.e. individual-focused interpretation)
    b. Crowd of fish was chasing the lone fish (i.e. community-focused interpretation)
    c. ish were a family with the father leading (i.e. patriarchal interpretation)

19. In 2004, subjects were unknowingly primed with the face of either a black or white male, then asked to identify weapons in a series of images. Regardless of their own race, subjects primed with the image of a black male were quicker to identify weapons. They were also more likely to incorrectly identify non-weapons as weapons. What do these results reveal about implicit associations and race?
    a. Cultural stereotypes are biologically rooted and beyond our control
    b. Implicit associations between race and expectations are innate
    c. Cultural stereotypes influence perceptions and actions without our awareness

20. What is the Implicit Association Test (IAT) designed to detect?
    a. Unconscious biases based on how quickly or slowly subjects associate certain words and images
    b. Conscious biases based on how quickly or slowly subjects associate certain words and images
    c. Unconscious biases based on pupillary dilation when exposed to certain images

CHAPTER V: SHAKESPEARE'S MAKEOVER: HAWT OR NAWT?

1.	True	11.	B
2.	True	12.	A
3.	True	13.	C
4.	False	14.	A
5.	True	15.	A
6.	A	16.	B
7.	C	17.	A
8.	C	18.	B
9.	A	19.	C
10.	B	20.	A

CHAPTER VI

CONSTRUCTING THE "OTHER"

Race & Ethnicity

"When I was in Africa, this voice came to me and said, 'Richard, what do you see?'.

I said, 'I see all types of people.'

The voice said, 'But do you see any niggers?'.

I said, 'No.'

It said, "Do you know why? 'Cause there aren't any."'

– Richard Pryor, Live at the Sunset Strip (1982)

For comedy icon Richard Pryor, life as a black man in the US was a wellspring of fodder. Throughout the 1970s, the word "nigger" figured prominently in his acts and album titles. But in 1979, a visit to Kenya changed his view of the word and its implications. According to his memoir, *Pryor Convictions*, the moment of insight struck while relaxing in the hotel lobby. Pryor saw that it was full of "gorgeous black people, like everyplace else we'd been. . . . the hotel, on television, in stores, on the street, in the newspapers, at restaurants, running the government, on advertisements. Everywhere." He then turned to his wife and said, "You know what? There are no niggers here." Pryor meant that since the word "nigger" was not a part of their culture, the concept had not been incorporated into black identity in Kenya. By adopting this word, he had accepted society's negative implications of what it meant to be black. For Pryor, being exposed to a different view of black identity in Kenya revealed how culturally limited his own perspective had been. When Pryor returned to the US, he expressed regret for "ever having uttered the word 'nigger' on a stage or off it. It was a wretched word. Its connotations weren't funny, even when people laughed . . . I vowed never to say it again."

Pryor's decision was lauded by some and criticized by others. Those in agreement felt that normalizing the slur only cemented its negative stereotypes in black self and social identity. On the other side of the debate, the word was seen as a tool of empowerment. In 1996, Def Jam founder Russell Simmons explained, "When we say 'nigger' now, it's very positive . . . When black kids call each other 'a real nigger' or 'my nigger,' it means you . . . have your own culture that you invent so you don't have to buy into the U.S. culture that you're not really a part of."[1] Although disagreement over the "n-word" remains, Pryor's decision and the ongoing debate reflect the role culture plays in defining race and ethnicity.

Race and ethnicity are culturally constructed categories, meaning that they are based on learned cultural beliefs, NOT objective scientific standards. **Race** is defined as *perceived* physical differences. **Ethnicity** refers to *perceived* cultural differences. "Perceived" is the key word in both of these definitions. It is often assumed

---

[1] Jackson, Derrick Z. "The N-word and Richard Pryor." *The New York Times*, December 15, 2005. Accessed April 27, 2017. http://www.nytimes.com/2005/12/15/opinion/the-nwordand-richard-pryor.html

that race and ethnicity refer to biological traits and/or geographic ancestry. On the contrary, racial and ethnic groups are actually a reflection of cultural, social, and political environments. We classify ourselves and each other based on *learned cultural beliefs*. How we are taught to organize the world affects our views of:

- Which groups exist
- Characteristics associated with each group
- Who belongs to each group
- Which group we think we belong to (self-identity)
- Which group other people think we belong to (social identity)

Race and ethnicity will be unpacked in three parts. Part I focuses on how definitions of race differ between cultures and transform through time. Part II discusses incongruent views of ethnicity and resulting conflicts. In Part III, we assess how these classifications have been used as tools of oppression and empowerment.

PART I: RACE

Race is generally defined as *perceived* <u>physical</u> differences. "Perceived" is the operative word because race is defined by <u>learned cultural beliefs</u>, NOT biology. Individuals categorized as members of the same race are *believed* to share a set of physical similarities. In this section, we will examine: 1) traits commonly (mis)used to define race; 2) how history shaped race in America; 3) Brazil's complex classification system.

A. WHAT DEFINES RACE?

Many people assume that race has a biological basis because visible, physical features are used to identify racial groups. However, scientific classification implies that all group members share a common set of characteristics. For example, all animals that are classified as mammals have mammary glands, fur, and a four-chambered heart. Whereas people identified as members of the same race often do not possess all or any traits used to define these groups. This is because which **race is a reflection of cultural beliefs, not scientific data.** In this section, we will examine the inaccuracy of the most common means of defining racial groups.

Skin color is the most common characteristic used to define racial categories, but there is no consistent range within which all members of a group fall. Consider the enormous variation among people identified in the US as black or white. This spectrum results in overlap between racial categories, such as individuals identified as black having lighter skin than those classified as white. Despite skin color often being situated as an integral factor in race, it is actually the least unreliable indicator.

Other physical features are often used in conjunction with skin color to define race. But like skin color, these traits do not appear consistently in all members classified as a racial group. One example of this is the epicanthic fold, a crease in the upper eyelid resulting in what some describe as an almond-shaped eye. This feature is associated with people who are racially classified as Asian. While this characteristic is common to people of Asian descent, it is not universal and appears with greater frequency among East Asian populations. The epicanthic fold also appears with in groups not identified as Asian, such as Africans and Scandinavians.

Geographic ancestry, or where an individual's ancestors came from, is sometimes used to signal racial identity. In the US, labels like "African American" and "Asian American" echo this belief. But people are often assigned to racial categories that do not reflect all or any of their actual geographic ancestry. Discrepancies stem from social hierarchies that elevate some lineages, while obscuring others. Consequently, racial systems based on presumed geographic ancestry are often incomplete or utterly inaccurate.

B. MISTAKEN IDENTITY

Racial Classification in the US

Wayne Joseph was a proud black man. He valued his African American identity and taught his children to honor theirs. As a school administrator and race relations writer, he emphasized the importance of celebrating heritage. But at the age of 51, Joseph was shocked to learn that his African roots did not exist.

The discovery came as a result of a DNA test designed to reveal where your ancestors came from. Some genetic sequences are only common or unique to specific geographic regions. If a person's DNA has this specific sequence, then their ancestors are most likely from this region. In an ABC News interview, Joseph recalled the moment, "I just glanced at it, just a cursory glance initially — didn't really notice it much. Then, I went back to it, because all of a sudden it hit me exactly what I had read . . . 57 percent Indo-European, 39 percent Native American, 4 percent East Asian and 0 percent African."

How did this happen? **In the US, race is based on visible characteristics and presumed geographic ancestry.** But as previously discussed, beliefs about ancestry are dictated by social hierarchy. Wayne Joseph's racial identity was a byproduct of America's segregationist history. When his ancestors arrived in 19th century Louisiana, cultural attitudes about white superiority were reinforced by segregation laws. Segregation laws enforced boundaries between whites and nonwhites in all aspects of life. Nonwhites had separate schools, restaurants, and units in the military. Romantic relationships with whites were deemed criminal. Joseph's ancestors were of predominantly European origin, but they were *socially identified* as white or nonwhite based on their complexions. Relatives with darker skin were subject to the **one-drop rule**, which classified individuals perceived as having <u>any</u> nonwhite ancestry as nonwhite. They were *socially identified* and treated as nonwhite. The ancestors who had been socially identified as white chose to identify as black. This choice was driven by not wanting to identify with a group whom they viewed as oppressors. It was also to avoid difficulties of dating people identified as nonwhite, such as not being allowed to eat in the same restaurants. The racial hierarchy of 19th century Louisiana led to Joseph's family actively rejecting their European ancestry and adopting the black racial identity. Consequently, a social identity assigned by others redefined the Joseph family's self-identity.

Segregation laws were ruled unconstitutional in the 1960s, but the one-drop rule remains entrenched in cultural tradition. Americans of mixed-race heritage, such as former President Barack Obama, are still referred to as black. Social identity influences the way we see ourselves. Being socially identified as black, President Obama expressed a strong sense of responsibility to African American communities. Social identity informs one's approach to race, as it did for the former president. It can also completely transform identities, as it did for Wayne Joseph.

C. IDENTITY CRISIS?

Racial Classification in Brazil

In a video posted by *The Globe and Mail*, Simone's family seems to be having an identity crisis.

"I'm *pardo*. That means mixed-race," explains her husband, Nei. Simone disagrees and states, "For me, there are only two races: white or black . . . I think Nei is black." Simone refers to herself as black. Her sister identifies as white.

"I think I am black. But people think I'm brown," says Simone's niece, Jessica. Appearing beside her in split screen, Simone's daughter declares, "My cousin Jessica is white. Her hair is straight." The video continues with Simone's family members identifying their races, then being contradicted by relatives.

Simone's family lives in Brazil, where a notoriously complicated system of race makes their situation quite common. It is solely based on physical characteristics, such as skin tone and hair texture. But as Simone's family demonstrates, there are conflicting views of which visible traits matter most. Beliefs about geographic ancestry are not a factor in racial identity, as they do in the US. This means that parents may identify their children as races other than their own.

To confuse matters even more, opinions differ over which racial categories even exist. In the 1970s, the *Brazilian Institute of Geography and Statistics* conducted a survey asking respondents in northeastern Brazil to describe their skin color. They received 134 different answers! Some responses highly specific, such as "white with brown spots" or "white like a meringue." Other descriptions bordered on prose. One description included the phrase "burro (donkey) running away." The agency that conducted this survey also organizes the national census every decade. Currently, the census lists five categories based on skin color: indigenous, yellow, white, pardo (brown) and preto (dark-skinned). Black is absent from the list. Like many others, Simone surely disagrees.

Racial classifications are bases on social stratification, or levels of inequality in society. How a culture conceptualizes race affects the rights and treatment of its members. Examining the consequences of different beliefs about race can allow us to avoid negative repercussions and emphasize positive outcomes.

PART II: ETHNICITY

Ethnicity refers to *perceived* <u>cultural</u> differences. Ethnic groups are viewed by themselves or others as sharing a unique cultural identity, such as similar norms, values, and beliefs. "Perceived" is the key word in this definition because what qualifies someone as a member of an ethnic group is a reflection of cultural beliefs.

The ethnic group with whom you identify may differ from how others categorize you. For example, my parents are originally from Vietnam, but they are American citizens. I was born and raised in the US. I'm embarrassed to admit that I can't fluently speak, read, or write in Vietnamese. Overall, I identify far more with American than Vietnamese culture. However, I am often referred to as Vietnamese when in the US. But when I'm in Asia, friends often refer to me as "the American." Ethnic identity may seem inconsequential in America's racialized social landscape. But in a nation comprised of immigrants, how we define our cultural identity informs our views and interactions. In my case, it results in being viewed as "Other" at home and abroad.

Cultural beliefs about the ethnic identity inform regulations that affect relationships between immigrants and their new communities. How groups define *their own* ethnic identity shapes what is required of immigrants seeking membership. For example, what a US citizen views as "being American" influences what this person believes immigrants must do in order to qualify for access to the nation's resources. This was also illustrated by France's controversial ban on women wearing full-face Muslim veils in public. Public opinions were divided based on beliefs about the role of Islam in French identity. Regulations to accept or reject facets of immigrant cultures inform how citizens view their roles in these communities. The core of this conflict is the struggle between assimilation and multiculturalism.

Assimilation refers to adopting mainstream culture, rather than trying to remain ethnically distinct. The primary advantage of assimilation is access to resources. For example, learning English in the US makes it easier to find employment. Some have proposed that assimilation contributes to a stronger sense of unity. A disadvantage of assimilation is that it inevitably leads to the loss or dilution of cultural knowledge. Consider how much cultural knowledge, such as language and culinary customs, you have retained from your family's ethnic history. It is likely that you do not have deep familiarity, if any, with the traditions of your ancestors. A practical problem with assimilation is determining what "mainstream" culture means. This issue is central to ongoing debates over France's ban on Muslim face coverings. Former Prime Minister François Fillon argued that face coverings prevented women from assimilating because it marked them as separate and inferior, qualities that did not align with French values of equality. Those opposed argued that the law violated religious freedom and stereotyped the practice as oppressive, which contributed to the stigmatization of French Muslims.

Multiculturalism supports the idea that variants from other cultures should be integrated into mainstream culture. This is demonstrated by the "melting pot" concept often used to describe the diversity of American culture. An advantage of multiculturalism is that it contributes to peaks in technological and cultural development. Varied perspectives support the influx of innovation. New York city serves as an example of the benefits of multiculturalism. Its history as a port city resulted in the concentrated convergence of a wide array of cultures. As a result, New York is widely viewed as a pinnacle of progress and cultural diversity. The downside of multiculturalism is that retaining too much distinctiveness can inhibit access to resources. This disadvantage is central to arguments against multilingual education in the US. Multilingual schools provide academic instruction in English and students' native languages. These programs are intended to offset learning lags due to language barriers, as well as help immigrant children preserve traditional culture. But opponents state that the lack of immersion actually hinders the rate at which students learn English. Many argue that time spent teaching material in native languages would be more effectively allotted to teaching English. Conflicting views of multilingual education have become a legislative battleground with immigrant families on both sides.

Establishing an effective combination of assimilation and multiculturalism is crucial to societal success. Immigrants must assimilate in order to survive and flourish in new cultural environments. Multiculturalism provides a catalyst for community progress and development. Thus, culturally-based legislation must be weighed with equal parts of practicality and empathy.

PART III: BLURRED LINES

The line that divides racial and ethnic identity is porous. Physical traits are sometimes used to describe ethnic groups, while cultural traditions may be linked to certain races. Classifications of race and ethnicity shift in response to social hierarchy, based on which traits are believed to represent insider status. Whether a group is defined as race or ethnicity has profound effects on how they are treated within a social system. The designation of race implies physical distinctiveness, which many misconstrue as biological differences. This view has been used to justify inhumane treatment based on the belief some individuals are subhuman. The ethnic group label infers a cultural separateness from the mainstream population, making it possible to frame them as a threat. The impacts of being defined alternately as a race and ethnicity are detailed in this section's examination of the Irish. The blurred boundary between these categories allows them to be redefined, sometimes as tools of oppression. However, the flexibility of these classifications also provides the opportunity to empower. In this section, we will explore varied effects of these culturally constructed categories.

A. THE MAN IN THE MONKEY CAGE

Ethnicity Redefined as Race

In September 1906, over 200,000 people flocked to see the newest exhibit at New York City's Bronx Zoo. Newspaper headlines describing the spectacle as "shocking" and "scandalous" did not disappoint. Inside the primate house, visitors peered into a cage through steel bars and found a young man staring back. Dressed in modern clothing, he was roughly the size of an average 12-year-old and had pointed, crocodile-like teeth. Hordes of up to 500 onlookers at a time crowded around the cage to gasp, gawk, and mock.[2] The sign affixed to his cage read:

The African Pygmy, Ota Benga

Age, 23 years. Height, 4 feet 11 inches.

Weight 103 pound. Brought from the Kasai River,

Congo Free State, South Central Africa,

By Dr. Samuel P Verner.

Exhibited each afternoon during September

The cage was not locked, but Ota faced relentless harassment by visitors and workers when he wandered the grounds. Attempts to defend himself or retaliate were reported as a primitive lack of self-control. Sometimes, he entertained patrons by shooting a target with the bow and arrow placed in his cage. When irritated, he mocked patrons by mimicking their hoots and jeers. This delighted the crowds, but not everyone was amused. A group of black clergymen led vigorous protests calling for termination of the offensive display. Their efforts succeeded and the spectacle ended after twenty days. But Ota's troubles did not end with the exhibit. It was neither the first nor the last time that racial and ethnic prejudice that would determine Ota's fate.

Ota was brought to the US after Belgian forces massacred his tribe and sold him at the slave market. Samuel Phillips Verner, an African explorer from the US, purchased Ota along with members of another pygmy tribe. When Verner went broke, he arranged for Ota to live and work at the Bronx Zoo. In less than a week, the director persuaded Ota to "perform" inside one of primate house's large, empty cages. He was encouraged to bare his teeth and rush the cage bars, giving the audience a thrill and confirming their beliefs in his "untamed" nature. Traits that Ota proudly viewed as part of his Mbuti ethnic identity were repackaged as indicators of subhuman savagery. His small stature, characteristic of all pygmy tribes, was presented as proof that African pygmies were the "missing link" between humans and apes. Ota's pointed teeth, filed in popular Mbuti fashion, were reduced to mere novelty when zookeepers lined his cage with bones to falsely suggest cannibalism. In this hot, muggy weekend in September, Ota Benga became "the man in the monkey house."

---

[2] Keller, Mitch. "The Scandal at the Zoo." *New York Times*, August 6, 2006. Accessed March 3, 2017. http://www.nytimes.com/2006/08/06/nyregion/thecity/06zoo.html

After the debacle at zoo, Ota was placed in an orphanage for several years before being adopted by a family in Virginia. For many years, Ota worked to assimilate and build a normal life. He took odd jobs, changed his name to Otto Bingo, and had his teeth capped. He befriended some of the neighborhood youths, teaching them to hunt, fish, and regaling them with stories of hunting large game in Africa. He was introduced to prominent African American figures, W.E.B. DuBois and Booker T. Washington. But these moments of joy were overshadowed by growing depression, exacerbated by the diminishing likelihood of returning to Africa due to lack of resources. Despite Ota's efforts to construct a new life in America, a decade of despondence finally proved to be too much. One afternoon in March 1916, Ota built a ceremonial fire, knocked the caps from his teeth, and shot himself in the chest.[3]

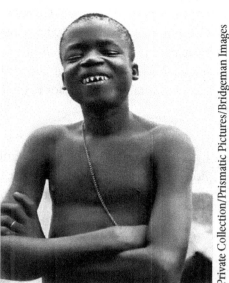

Private Collection/Prismatic Pictures/Bridgeman Images

Ota's story serves as a chilling caveat about the potentially devastating effects of cultural beliefs about race and ethnicity. Racial and ethnic discrimination did not only give rise to this exhibit: they shaped his entire life. Ota's cage was not constructed of concrete and steel; rather, it was constructed by culture. Ultimately, his life was constrained by perceptions about who he was and who he had the right to become.

B. NO IRISH NEED APPLY

Race or Ethnicity?

In 19th century Europe, the Irish were viewed as an inferior RACE. At this time, the idea that some groups of people represented earlier stages of evolution was supported by a large portion of the scientific community. In 1862, prominent anthropologist Dr. John Beddoe published an anatomical analysis of the Irish

GROCERY CART AND HARNESS FOR SALE
—In good order, and one chestnut horse, 8 years old, an excellent saddle horse; can be ridden by a lady   Also, one young man wanted, from 16 to 18 years of age, able to write No Irish need apply. CLUFF & TUNIS, No. 270 Washington-st., corner of Myrtle-av., Brooklyn.

NEW YORK DAILY TIMES, MARCH 25, 1854.

in which he claimed that their physical features were evidence that they were more closely related to early humans. He concluded that this predisposed the Irish to having lower IQ's leading to higher rates of deviance and criminality. This led to views of the Irish as physically distinct, inferior, and worthy of discrimination.

In the early 1800s, large groups of Irish immigrants arriving in the US were viewed as an inferior ETHNICITY. Racially categorized as white, they were not subject to segregationist laws imposed on nonwhites. However, discrimination still impeded their access to employment and education. Stereotypes of the Irish as drunkards, welfare scammers, and criminals made for an unwelcoming job market. Postings commonly included the phrase, "No Irish Need Apply".[4] Archival data reveals that the New York Sun published 15 of these advertisements in just one year.[5] Prejudice was also aimed at their Catholicism, viewed as a radical religion by America's Protestant majority. Many believed that their loyalty to the Pope, a foreign leader, weakened

[3] Newkirk, Pamela. *Spectacle: The Astonishing Life of Ota Benga.* New York: HarperCollins/Amistad, 2015.

[4] Bulik, Mark. "1854: No Irish Need Apply." *New York Times*, September 8, 2015. Accessed March 1, 2017. https://www.nytimes.com/2015/09/08/insider/1854-no-irish-need-apply.html

[5] Fried, Rebecca A. "No Irish Need Deny: Evidence for the Historicity of NINA Restrictions in Advertisements and Signs." *Journal of Social History* 49, no. 4 (Summer 2016): 829–854.

their allegiance to the US. Growing religious backlash prompted the Irish to develop a network of private Catholic schools in an effort to shield their children from evangelical and sectarian messaging in the public system. In response, an amendment barring state funding for private schools was adopted in thirty states and left Catholic schools struggling for financial support. Systematic bias in employment and education was an insurmountable obstacle for many Irish Americans.

During the 1900s, persistent poverty made the Irish a target of horrific eugenics policies. Eugenics, derived from a Greek word meaning "good birth," is the belief that undesirable traits can be removed from society by preventing "defective" people from reproducing. The eugenics movement was based on faulty interpretations of scientific principles, which led to misguided theories linking genetics to social problems. Beginning in 1907, over thirty states approved legislation supporting forced sterilization of "defective" individuals to prevent them from reproducing. Traits used to identify "defectives" were common to negative stereotypes of the poor, such as being promiscuous or uneducated. These traits were incorrectly attributed to genetics, making poverty itself a sign of biological deficiency. Since impoverished communities were largely comprised of minorities and immigrants, this theory validated existing cultural beliefs about their inferiority. **It also resurrected views of the Irish as a biologically inferior race, qualifying them as "defectives" and vulnerable to eugenics policies.** These policies did not fall out of favor until the 1940s, by which time over 60,000 US citizens had been sterilized through coercion.

Struggles created by views of Irish Americans as Other also transformed how the community saw itself. Efforts to assimilate into the mainstream while maintaining tradition produced a unique Irish American identity. Customs created in an effort to honor the homeland often differed from their original forms. An example of this is celebrating St. Patrick's Day, a staple of Irish American culture. In Ireland, it was a somber day of attending church. During the 19th century, Irish immigrants would commemorate the occasion with small celebrations. By comparison, the raucous partying associated with the holiday in the US today is unrecognizable. Irish American identity is as complicated as the history from which it was borne. It also demonstrates the immense influence of cultural beliefs on self and social identity.

C. TURNING JAPANESE

Redefining Race and Ethnicity

On March 12, 2015, Ariana Miyamoto made international headlines as the first biracial winner of Miss Universe Japan. The leggy, 21-year-old model would represent Japan in the Miss Universe pageant. With the exception of Miyamoto's racial status, everything else seemed like standard pageant fare. After being crowned, a neatly coiffed host presented Miyamoto with a sash. Other contestants stood behind her smiling and applauding. But as she stood on the runway beaming and wiping away tears of joy, a firestorm of controversy was brewing outside.

Amid the cheers of racial progress from many, questions arose of whether or not Miyamoto was "Japanese enough" to represent the nation. One person criticized the win online in a post reading, "Shouldn't the Japanese Miss

Universe at least have a Japanese face?"[6] Criticisms reflected the belief that to qualify as "real Japanese," one must have cultural fluency *and* specific physical traits. **Traits used to define race and ethnicity often overlap, making the difference between these categories unclear.** In Japan, race and ethnicity are intertwined. Citizens of mixed race are referred to as "hafu", meaning "half," and often face discrimination for not being "real Japanese." Miyamoto's mother is Japanese and her father is African American. When she was very young, he returned to the US and Miyamoto was raised in Japan. Although Miyamoto **self-identified** as Japanese, she was **socially identified** as a hafu and teased for being an outsider. As a child, classmates called her "kurombo", the Japanese version of the "n-word." Others avoided physical contact fearing that her color would rub off on their skin. This made Miyamoto's victory a coup in the face of traditional cultural identity.

At thirteen, Miyamoto lived with her father in Arkansas and attended two years of high school. Her racial identity was redefined in the American cultural system as black. In Japan, the hafu label was isolating. It meant that she was racially distinct from everyone, including her parents. But in the US, identifying as black emphasized connection to her father's side of the family. It gave her a sense of belonging and community. As she stated in a *New York Times* interview, "They had the same skin and face as me. For the first time, I felt normal." Miyamoto noted that in contrast to the narrow definition of Japanese identity, a wider range of races were accepted as American. This experience helped lay the groundwork for what would become her life's mission.

Miyamoto returned to Japan with a new perspective, but unsure of its implementation. The suicide of a friend brought her mission into focus. Miyamoto's friend killed himself after a lifetime of being bullied for being mixed-race. This inspired her to represent people of mixed-race as deserving of acceptance and recognition in Japan. Miyamoto entered the Miss Universe Japan competition, which is largely based on physical appearance, as a statement of pride in mixed race heritage. Miyamoto's victory inspired Priyanka Yoshikawa, who is of Indian and Japanese descent, to pursue her dreams. After being crowned Miss World Japan 2016, she told the BBC, "Before Ariana, hafu girls couldn't represent Japan. That's what I thought too. Ariana encouraged me a lot by showing me and all mixed girls the way."

Miyamoto's story provides a message of hope that resonates beyond Japan's borders. Our biological instinct to form groups is inescapable, but the cultural beliefs we use to define these groups are malleable. It may be impossible to eradicate the practice of sorting people based on race and ethnicity, but we can decide what these categories mean. Perceptions of ourselves and others can determine the obstacles you face, as well the opportunities you are afforded. We can allow imagined boundaries to divide and oppress, or construct identities that unify and empower.

---

[6] Fackler, Martin. "Biracial Beauty Queen Challenges Japan's Self-Image." *New York Times*, May 29, 2015. Accessed March 1, 2017. https://www.nytimes.com/2015/05/30/world/asia/biracial-beauty-queen-strives-for-change-in-mono-ethnic-japan.html?_r=0

PRACTICE EXAM QUESTIONS
CHAPTER VI: CONSTRUCTING THE "OTHER"

T F 1.   Racial categories are based on <u>actual biological differences</u>.

T F 2.   <u>Ethnicity</u> refers to <u>perceived cultural differences</u>.

T F 3.   Racial classifications are based on <u>social stratification</u>, or levels of inequality in society.

T F 4.   <u>Multiculturalism</u> means to adopt mainstream culture, rather than remaining ethnically distinct.

T F 5.   Ariana Miyamoto <u>self-identifies</u> as Japanese, but is <u>socially identified</u> as a foreigner.

6.   During a visit to Kenya, Richard Pryor said, "There are no niggers here." What did he mean?
   a.   Negative stereotypes associated with the word were not part of black identity in Kenya.
   b.   He only applied the term to poor black people, none of whom were in the wealthy city he visited.
   c.   He was commenting on the injustice of black Kenyans not being allowed into tourist areas.

7.   What argument did Russell Simmons present in support of using the "n-word"?
   a.   Hearing the word regularly could desensitize young African Americans to its effects.
   b.   The word was a reminder of oppression and social injustice experienced by African Americans.
   c.   It had been redefined in a positive way and provided a unique cultural identity for African Americans.

8.   Why is "perceived" a key word in definitions of race and ethnicity?
   a.   Categories are based on what people can <u>physically see</u>, or visually perceive.
   b.   They are <u>culturally constructed categories</u> based on perceptions of what make groups distinct.
   c.   Categories are based on <u>genetic and anatomical traits</u> that can be perceived with scientific testing.

9.   Why is skin color is an <u>inaccurate</u> indicator of race?
   a.   It is not consistently applied to members identified as the same race.
   b.   Skin color can be changed by sun exposure, cosmetics, and artificial tanning.
   c.   Scientific studies show that skin color changes as individuals age.

10.   Why are physical features an <u>inaccurate</u> indicator of race?
   a.   They are not found in all individuals identified as the same race.
   b.   Features used to define race vary between cultures.
   c.   All of the above.

11.   What does the Wayne Joseph case demonstrate?
   a.   Racial identity often <u>does not</u> accurately reflect geographic ancestry.
   b.   Geographic ancestry is the <u>most accurate</u> indicator of race.
   c.   Geographic ancestry <u>and</u> physical features are an accurate indicator of race.

12.   Why did Wayne Joseph identify as African American?
   a.   He was raised by his African American mother and never knew his European father.
   b.   Under the one-drop rule, his ancestors were socially identified as black.
   c.   DNA testing revealed that 75% of his ancestry was African.

13. According to the one-drop rule, what classifies an individual as nonwhite?
    a. Any amount of nonwhite ancestry
    b. 50% nonwhite ancestry (i.e. one nonwhite parent)
    c. 25% nonwhite ancestry (e.g. one nonwhite grandparent)

14. What is the significance of the one-drop rule?
    a. It was the first DNA-based definition of race in the US.
    b. It restricted segregation laws to individuals with more than 25% nonwhite ancestry.
    c. Being classified as nonwhite meant being subjected to segregation laws.

15. How does Brazil's racial classification system differ from the US?
    a. It is based solely on presumed geographic ancestry.
    b. It is based solely on physical characteristics.
    c. It is based on skin color and geographic ancestry.

16. What does *The Globe and Mail*'s video about Simone's family say about race in Brazil?
    a. Beliefs about which traits define race often vary between individuals.
    b. Racial classification is more consistent in Brazil than in the US.
    c. Racial classification is more consistent in the US than in Brazil.

17. Which concept is demonstrated by France's controversial ban on Muslim women wearing veils?
    a. Beliefs about ethnic identity inform laws that affect relationships between immigrants and their new communities.
    b. Differing beliefs about ethnic identity, such as the role of Islam in French identity, can lead to conflict.
    c. All of the above.

18. Which of the following demonstrates an <u>advantage</u> of <u>assimilation</u>?
    a. Bilingual education providing lessons in immigrants' native languages to offset learning lags.
    b. Incorporating variants from other cultures to accelerate technological and social progress.
    c. Immigrants from non-English speaking countries learning English to access more jobs.

19. How does France's controversial ban on full-face veils demonstrate a <u>disadvantage</u> of <u>assimilation</u>?
    a. Conflicting views of ethnic identity make it difficult to determine what "mainstream" culture means.
    b. Adopting mainstream culture makes it easier to access resources.
    c. Retaining too much cultural distinctiveness makes it difficult to access resources.

20. Which of the following demonstrates an <u>advantage</u> of <u>multiculturalism</u>?
    a. Immigrants from non-English speaking countries learning English to access more jobs.
    b. Multilingual education providing lessons in immigrants' native languages to offset learning lags.
    c. Muslim women in France no longer wearing face veils to demonstrate support for traditional values.

21. How do arguments <u>against</u> multilingual education demonstrate a <u>disadvantage</u> of <u>multiculturalism</u>?
    a. Conflicting views of ethnic identity make it difficult to determine what "mainstream" culture means.
    b. Adopting mainstream culture makes it easier to access resources.
    c. Retaining too much cultural distinctiveness makes it difficult to access resources.

22. How did Ota Benga's self and social identities differ in the US?
    a. He <u>self-identified</u> as a member of the <u>Mbuti ethnic group</u>.
        He was <u>socially identified</u> as an <u>inferior race</u>.
    b. He <u>self-identified</u> as a member of the <u>pygmy racial group</u>.
        He was <u>socially identified</u> as a member of the <u>Mbuti ethnic group</u>.
    c. He <u>self-identified</u> as a member of the <u>Mbuti ethnic group</u>.
        He was socially identified as an <u>American citizen</u>.

23. Why were the Irish discriminated against in <u>19th century Europe</u>?
    a. They were viewed as a physically distinct and inferior race.
    b. Their Catholicism was seen as a threat to democracy.
    c. They were viewed as an inferior ethnic group whose vulgar traditions disrupted social order.

24. Why were Irish immigrants discriminated against in the US during the 19th century?
    a. Their Catholicism was seen as a threat to American democracy.
    b. They were viewed as an inferior ethnic group whose vulgar traditions disrupted social order.
    c. All of the above

25. During the eugenics movement, poverty was deemed to be a sign of biological defectiveness. How did this affect Irish American communities?
    a. It fueled views of the Irish as an <u>inferior ethnicity</u>, making them targets of eugenics policies.
    b. It resurrected views of the Irish as an <u>inferior race</u>, making them targets of eugenics policies.
    c. It fueled views of the Irish as a <u>superior race</u>, a belief that shielded them from eugenics policies.

26. Which concept is demonstrated by controversy over Ariana Miyamoto's Japanese identity?
    a. Traits used to define race and ethnicity often overlap; the difference between these categories unclear.
    b. Self-identity is more powerful than social identity in Japan.
    c. Race is more important than ethnicity in Japan.

27. How does being socially identified as a hafu affect Ariana Miyamoto?
    a. She is treated as a higher social class because of her "exotic" foreign heritage.
    b. She is viewed as a foreigner and faces discrimination for not being "true" Japanese.
    c. She is discriminated against for being "pure" Japanese.

28. Which concept is demonstrated by the Ota Benga, Irish, and Ariana Miyamoto cases?
    a. Race and ethnicity are unclear, yet consequential categories.
    b. Scientific definitions of race can be used to end ethnic discrimination.
    c. Race is scientifically defined, whereas ethnicity is culturally constructed.

CHAPTER VI: CONSTRUCTING THE "OTHER"

1.	False	15.	B
2.	True	16.	A
3.	True	17.	A
4.	False	18.	C
5.	True	19.	A
6.	A	20.	B
7.	C	21.	C
8.	B	22.	A
9.	A	23.	A
10.	C	24.	C
11.	A	25.	B
12.	B	26.	A
13.	A	27.	B
14.	C	28.	A